THIS USED TO BE NASHVILLE

JAMES HOOBLER

Reedy Press
PO Box 5131
St. Louis, MO 63139
www.reedypress.com

Library of Congress Control Number: 2021935128

ISBN: 9781681063423

Front cover: Postcard images are from the personal collection of Jim Hoobler.

Printed in the United States of America
22 23 24 25 26   5 4 3 2 1

DEDICATION

I wish to dedicate this book to those who led the way over the past half century in helping to preserve a place for the past in our present, and hopefully into the future.

Among these heroes: Margaret Lindsley Warden, who was a founder of the Metropolitan Historical Commission of Nashville and Davidson County; May Dean Eberling, its first director; Charles Waterfield, FAIA, lover of historic architecture; Catherine Avery, who helped keep First Presbyterian Church from being demolished for a parking garage site; Fletch Coke, who helped to save Union Station and Second Avenue; and all the people working to revive these historic districts and neighborhoods.

CONTENTS

ACKNOWLEDGMENTS

I wish to thank Myers Brown, Tennessee State Library & Archives, for providing the image of the University of Nashville from the 1832 J. P. Ayres map of Nashville. I had figured out that the Rutledge-Middleton home, Rose Hill, appeared on it, and that this is the only known image of the home. The Rutledges were an incredibly important couple in the early years of Nashville, and the fact that a remnant of their home still stands is amazing.

John Guider, professional photographer extraordinaire, then zoomed in on the area of the engraving that I needed and enhanced it for me. He photographed my collection of historic postcards and a stereograph slide as well. He is a true friend and colleague.

I want to thank all the sites that helped me gain access, in particular Tori Mason with the Nashville Zoo at Grassmere and Brickey Nuchols at Glen Leven. They went above and beyond in helping me to find the right clear day, and time of day, to photograph their sites.

All current photographs were made by the author.

I also wish to thank Barbara Northcott and Jill Eccher, who helped to shepherd me through the editing of this book and its production process. They were very easy to work with and helped to guide me through the process.

INTRODUCTION

2020 was a wretched year. Nashville had a tornado that destroyed some buildings and severely damaged others. Then within a few weeks COVID-19 struck and shut down the planet. On Christmas Day a deranged bomber blew himself up in an explosion that ripped the façades off of four historic buildings on the longest stretch of 19th-century architecture in town and significantly damaged many others. The boarded-up windows are still apparent from both the tornado and the bomber. But Nashville is resilient. We are rebuilding, and the construction boom that began about a decade ago is still going on. AllianceBernstein moved to Nashville from New York. Amazon is hiring 5,000 people and building twin office towers. Oracle is moving here from Silicon Valley. We keep expanding, but we also are trying to save what makes us unique. Part of that is our architecture from the past. Look through these pages and see some of what sets Nashville and its people apart. Learn about our nearly 250 years of history, and come and enjoy our warm hospitality, great cuisine, fabulous broad spectrum of music, and rich history. You just might find a place that you could call home.

Nashville Wharf/ Riverfront Park

One of the first public green spaces in downtown Nashville was this mini oasis on the river bluff, at the present location of a representation of Fort Nashborough. The new Sparkman Street or Shelby Street bridge, which opened in 1909, is seen in the distance. Below the bluff to the right was the City Wharf. Riverboats tied up there from 1819 into the 1920s and local paddlewheel excursion boats have operated there from the 1960s to the present. Today the *General Jackson* showboat does lunch and dinner cruises on the river. Visitors and locals alike have enjoyed these cruises since 1985.

The Cumberland River was one of the main reasons Nashville was settled and developed. It was easier after the first riverboat was brought to Nashville in 1819, by William Carroll, to ship people and goods in and out of the settlement. Carroll was a local businessman, soldier, and politician. He served as Tennessee governor from 1821 to 1827, when term limits put him out of office. Eligible again in 1829, he was reelected and served until 1835.

The wharf saw a huge influx of soldiers, war material, and commercial traffic during the Civil War. This boom continued following the war up until railroads began to really compete with riverboats following that war. One of the men who profited from this river trade was Thomas Green Ryman, who ran a steamship line on the river. He lived in a large home on College Hill (now

THIS USED TO BE: The Nashville Wharf

NOW IT'S: Riverfront Park

LOCATION: The Cumberland River bank at the foot of Broadway

This is where Nashville got its start. The river brought the settlers here and then became a route for commerce for the city. The first image of the area is from around 1900. Now it is the site of a re-creation of the original fort, and a waterfront park for gatherings and concerts.

called Rutledge Hill), looking down on the river. He started his river business as a teen by catching fish in the river and selling them to Union troops in Occupied Nashville. He raised the money to build a revival hall, now Ryman Auditorium, which was renamed in his honor after his death.

Enjoy seasonal concerts on the riverfront, or bring a picnic and enjoy the view.

Nashville Wharf/ Fort Nashborough Park

Native Americans were drawn here by the rich mineral springs that bubbled up where the Bicentennial Capitol Mall State Park is located today, and they even had a mineral salts production facility located there. Those springs attracted buffalo, deer, bear, and many other game animals, and people naturally followed: first Native Americans, then fur trappers—both French and English—and finally European American settlers coming over the mountains from the East. The latter met with resistance from the Native peoples in wars that lasted from 1780 to 1794 and nearly pushed the colonists out of the Cumberland Basin. But by 1794 the new settlers had prevailed, and their settlement was secure.

The people who moved to the Bluffs on the Cumberland had walked here from Fort Patrick Henry in the winter of 1779. They arrived at the Bluff on Christmas Day and began to make claims to the land. Some families established blockhouse forts at a distance from the Bluff, and others, with lands nearer the river, built Fort Nashborough. It had cabins as part of the exterior fort walls, along with some blockhouse corner structures. It ran parallel to the present Church Street up the hill away from the Bluff.

In the first postcard image you can see the 1930 re-creation of Fort Nashborough by the Daughters of the American Revolution. Lizzie Elliott was one of the leaders in the effort to promote local history and had written *Early History of Nashville* in 1911. Women were some of the strongest advocates for the City Beautiful movement

THIS USED TO BE: Part of the municipal river landing area, and then a small park on the river bluff

NOW IT'S: A simulation of a frontier log fort

LOCATION: River Bluff north of Riverfront Park

The first frontier fort was near this spot. This re-creation gives visitors a sense of how dangerous those first 15 years of settlement were, with near constant attacks by the Indigenous peoples. The Daughters of the American Revolution built a re-creation in the 1930s, and it was rebuilt again recently.

in the early 20th century, and they were also prominent in promoting historic preservation and study.

In the posctcard you can see two riverboats tied up at the wharf, and in the upper right the River Freight Terminal. This large concrete structure stands in the river and was connected to the Tennessee Central Railroad line so that goods could be shipped by river or rail from that location. In 1981 Mayor Richard Fulton launched the creation of Riverfront Park to reconnect the city to its origins. The terminal was demolished down to the river level, and that became the base for new decking along the river. Grass and stepped terracing for gatherings and concerts were built down to the Cumberland.

Check out the interpretive signage and listen to nashvillesites.org free tours of areas around the city.

Acme Farm Supply Building

The area south of Broadway lies in a floodplain, and so has historically been an undesirable location. Paralleling the Cumberland River and going up Broadway to Fifth Avenue, and then up to Rutledge Hill, this area was a squalid slum. Yet on Rutledge Hill, old College Hill, lived a number of prominent families connected with the University of Nashville, and then Peabody College. Vanderbilt University had the Litterer Laboratory across Second Avenue from the university and a dental school up on the hill. Yet the neighborhood was near the wharf, which attracted riverboat crews looking for gambling, liquor, cheap accommodations, and prostitution. This led the area to be inhabited by poor people, including African Americans, poor whites, Irish and Jewish immigrants, and other groups struggling to survive. Periodically there would be talk of clearing out the area, and a new hay market was one of the first attempts to do that. Sol Cohen ran a "barrelhouse" here, where he had barrels of whiskey up on racks, with wooden spigots to draw off the liquor into bottles for his bartenders to serve or for customers to take home. This bar was called "The Bucket of Blood" due to its rough clientele. Next, the Sparkman Street/ Shelby Street bridge was built and cleared out some of the area. In 1905 one indignant citizen wrote to the *American* newspaper that the area was "a conglomeration of dives, brothels, pawn-shops, second-hand clothing stores, filthy habitations . . . accompanied by the daily display of lewdness and drunkenness on the sidewalks redolent with the stench of every vile odor . . . no city in America or Europe can

THIS USED TO BE: Acme Farm Supply

NOW IT'S: Acme Feed and Seed, a bar and restaurant

LOCATION: 101 Broadway

A great spot for a meal and a drink, looking down from the rooftop at the river and Lower Broad.

present a more disgraceful or sickening aspect of modern civilization." It was known as Black Bottom for the rich flood soil, but it was one of Nashville's worst slums.

Built around 1890, this building operated from 1907 as a farm supply store. You could buy straw, feed, wire, tools, or just about anything that a farmer might need. It was conveniently located near both the river and rail connections bringing in whatever they could sell from this location. One of the things that I remember about the 1980s was the very popular "dog dip Saturday." You could bring your pet in, and they would immerse it in a chemical flea and tick bath for you. Today Tom Morales operates Acme Feed and Seed as a multilevel restaurant and bar with a great view of the river and Broadway from its rooftop patio.

Merchants Hotel

Located in "Black Bottom," a notorious slum filled with bars, brothels, gambling dens, and cheap accommodations, this area was targeted for gentrification at the turn of the 20th century. The South Nashville Women's Federation, a group begun by the Centennial Club, lobbied for a city bond issue to underwrite a large park and a new bridge across the river. A large portion of the slums were demolished south of Broadway. The bridge was built, displacing many poor families. Warehouses and industries moved into the area, and it began to change. Built in 1892 as a place for traveling businessmen to stay, the Merchants Hotel is now a three-story restaurant. When it was being renovated, letters from the Civil War were found in the walls from someone who had stayed there decades after the war. They are framed and displayed today in one of the dining areas.

This was one of the early renovations on Lower Broadway, about a century after the building was erected. By the 1970s the Grand Ole Opry was leaving downtown for a new suburban theme park (since demolished for Opry Mills shopping center). The area had become more and more run-down. Peep shows and other less-reputable establishments were crowding out the furniture stores that had been popular in the area. With the opening of Riverfront Park as a new beginning, the area began to clean up and revive. Today it is a huge tourist magnet, with individual entertainers operating their own themed bars and restaurants from Rep. John Lewis Way to the park. On weekends it is filled with visitors barhopping, enjoying live Nashville music, and visiting such nearby sites as the Ryman Auditorium, the National Museum of African American Music, and the Country Music Hall of Fame and Museum.

THIS USED TO BE: Merchants Hotel

NOW IT'S: Merchants Hotel restaurant and bar

LOCATION: 401 Broadway

Traveling salesmen, steamboat passengers, and others passing through town could spend the night here, near the Wharf. The Broadway Drug Company used the ground-floor street corner. Now it is a fine restaurant and bar.

Ernest Tubb Record Shop

Ernest Tubb Record Shop has been on this site for over 70 years. Its *Midnite Jamboree* is the second-oldest continuously broadcast radio program in the United States. Following the late show at the Grand Ole Opry on Saturday night, performers would walk over to the record shop to perform and to sell their records. Patsy Cline, Carl Perkins, Johnny Cash, and Loretta Lynn have all performed here. It is still going on today, as the buildings at 417 to 423 Broadway are all music clubs and bars. Scenes from the film *Coal Miner's Daughter* were filmed here too.

The buildings date back to the 1850s, when William Stockell had an ornamental plaster business there. He did the plasterwork at the Tennessee State Capitol and at Belmont Mansion.

During the Civil War, this building was part of US Hospital No. 3, which had 250 beds for the care of wounded and sick Federal troops brought into the city from battlefields in Middle Tennessee. This was the first war in which the wounded received battlefield care, and that happened in Tennessee in April 1862, at the Battle of Shiloh. Railroads were newly employed to transport the wounded to hospitals. Embalming also was introduced during the Civil War, and William R. Cornelius was the local undertaker who had the government contract to care for Federal dead during the war. He helped with the new US Military Cemeteries interments at Nashville, Stones River, Shiloh, and Chattanooga, and trained Prince Greer, the first African American mortician to learn embalming. When General George Thomas was asked at Chattanooga whether the dead should be buried by state, he

Go inside and look at the old record sleeves of some of the musical legends who performed here after the last evening show at the Ryman.

Since 1947 this has been home to the *Midnite Jamboree*, which is the second-longest-running radio show in history. Many stars got their starts here.

answered, "No, mix them all up. I'm sick of states' rights." In Nashville, 21 different hospital complexes were set up, made up of buildings seized by the Federal government for the care of these men.

THIS USED TO BE: Stockell Ornamental Plasterers

NOW IT'S: Ernest Tubb Record Shop, Nashville Crossroads "Music City," Alan Jackson's Good Time Bar, and Mellow Mushroom

LOCATION: 417–423 Broadway

Friedman's Pawn Shop

The Second Fiddle honky-tonk is in the old Friedman's Pawn Shop. Musicians used to pawn their possessions here to get through the lean times while trying to get started in the music business.

Here there is live music seven days a week. The walls are lined with music memorabilia, along with old radios. These radios date back to when WSM Radio's clear broadcasts could be heard in most of the eastern United States, and families would tune in to hear the Grand Ole Opry in their living rooms.

Friedman's was the anchor for this end of Broadway, staying in the family as a pawn shop from 1923 to 2000. Part of the space was sublet from time to time, however. From 1956 to 1957 Reavis Recording Studio used space here. In 1958-60 it was Fidelity Recordings. Then from 1961 to 1970 Globe Recording was in that space. That extra space was vacant in 1971, but in 1972-73 Open Door Coffee House leased the space. With the Grand Ole Opry moving out to Opryland in 1974, the area went into a steep decline. In 1975 the Magic Fingers Massage Parlor opened, and in 1977 it became more explicit in its name and was called Sugar Shack Massage Parlor. It was shut down fairly quickly. Robert's Western World moved in in 2000, Rocky Top Saloon in 2001-2002, and finally Second Fiddle in 2003.

THIS USED TO BE: Friedman's Pawn Shop

NOW IT'S: Second Fiddle honky-tonk

LOCATION: 420 Broadway

The pawn shop where hungry musicians could pawn something until they saw better days.

Tootsie's Orchid Lounge

Hattie Louise "Tootsie" Bess ran Tootsie's Orchid Lounge beginning in 1960. Such performers as Willie Nelson, Kris Kristofferson, Faron Young, and Roger Miller were fed and "watered" there as they started out as struggling musicians. Tootsie had a heart of gold and went out of her way to help her "boys." Go out the back door, and you can see the door that Opry performers used to come in through from the stage door of the Ryman Auditorium across the back alley. After a visit to Tootsie's, the audience and the performers at the Opry were both a bit more lively.

This is pretty much the original honky-tonk in Nashville. Downstairs the Wall of Fame is lined with autographed photos of people who performed here. Scenes from the film *Coal Miner's Daughter* were filmed here as well.

In 1926 Morris and Fannie Stein opened a dry-goods store here. They continued to own the building but leased it out as Bob's Bicycle Shop in 1949-51. Then Cathey Paint & Wallpaper Co. rented here. John & Louise Café moved in from 1956 to 1958, and then Bill's Place from 1959 to 1960. In 1960 Hattie Louise opened it as her own honky-tonk.

THIS USED TO BE: A dry-goods store

NOW IT'S: Tootsie's Orchid Lounge

LOCATION: 422 Broadway

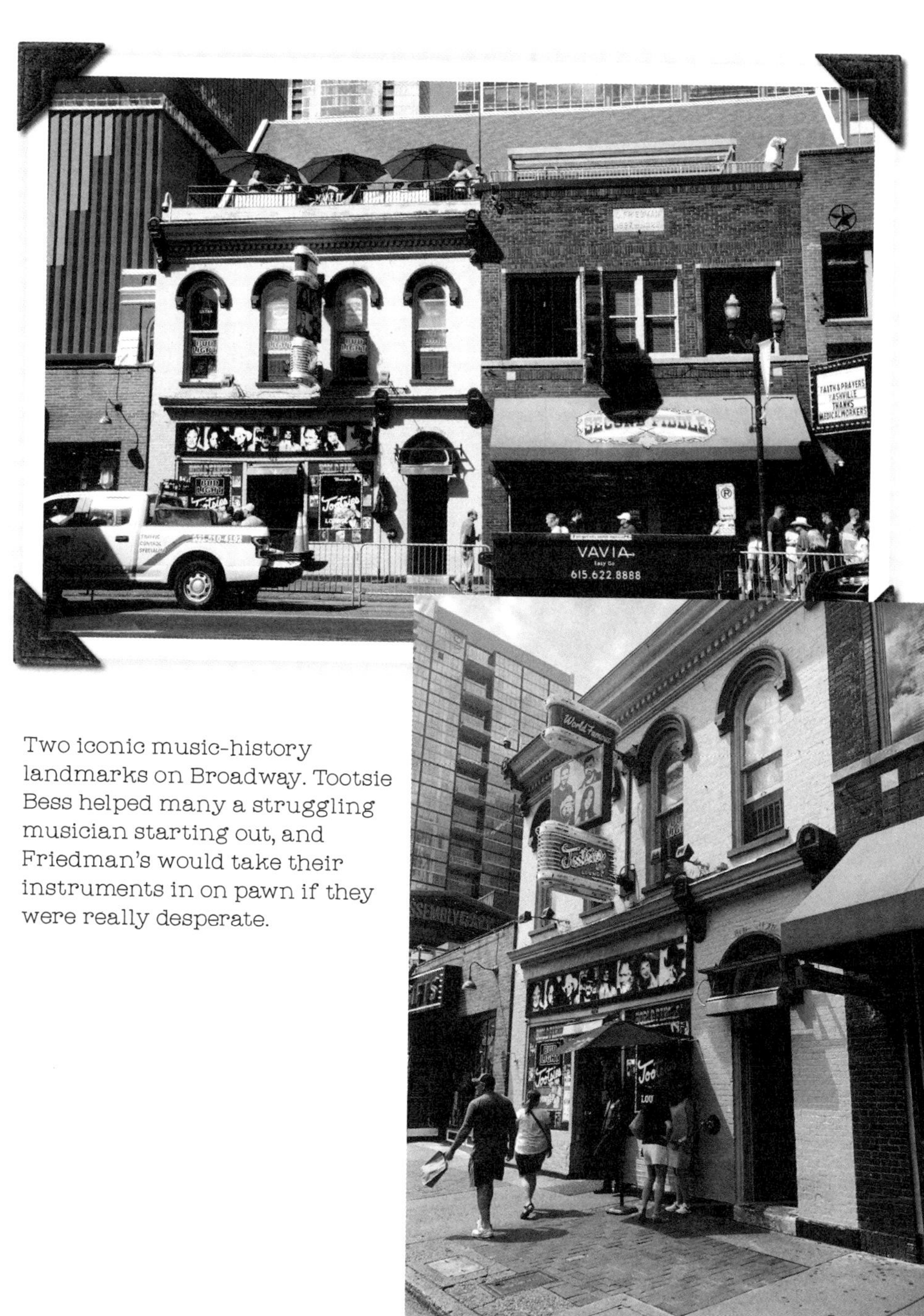

Two iconic music-history landmarks on Broadway. Tootsie Bess helped many a struggling musician starting out, and Friedman's would take their instruments in on pawn if they were really desperate.

Federal Style House

This is the oldest surviving house in downtown Nashville. Built around 1820 by the McCann family, it was a typical middle-class home of that period. The traditional two-story, three-bay house is in a plain style popular at the time it was built. When a friend was renovating the building, I asked him whether there was a basement. He checked under the flooring, and sure enough there was—with river silt in it from the many times the Cumberland had flooded this far up Broadway.

In about 1880 the commercial structure next door, at 106 Rep. John Lewis Way (Fifth Avenue South), was built. The ground floor was a business, and the second floor a residence. In 1994 both floors were adapted for retail and restaurant space.

Haralson-Eagun Tire & Vulcanizing Company occupied this house in 1926 and, in 1930, H. E. Slack Novelty Company Printers worked from here. From 1942 to 1944, it was the Hughes Barber Shop. In 1946 it transitioned into Morgan W. Brown Radio Repair; in 1949, it was H. D. Harell 2nd Hand Goods; in 1951, James Grady restaurant; in 1958, J & B Café; and from 1959 to 1961, it was Virgie's Café. From 1962 to 1963, it was Russell's Tavern, in 1965 No Return, from 1966 to 1967 Fifth Avenue Tap Room, in 1968 Say When Lounge Tavern, and in 1969 it was vacant. From 1970 to 1971, it was the Hen's Tail Tavern, from 1972 to 2000 Say When Lounge, in 2001 Bogey's Sports Souvenirs, Honky Tonk Heart Cafeteria, and Turnberry Associates. From 2002 to 2005, it was AAA Tix ticket service and Bogey's, in 2007 Wild Bill's Restaurant, and is now a Mexican restaurant.

THIS USED TO BE: A circa 1820 home

NOW IT'S: Pancho & Lefty's Cantina

LOCATION: 104 5th Ave. S. (Rep. John Lewis Way)

The oldest surviving house downtown, this is now Pancho & Lefty's Cantina.

Rose Hill

Rose Hill was the home of Henry Middleton Rutledge and Septima Sexta Middleton Rutledge. They were first cousins and the children of Edward Rutledge and Arthur Middleton, South Carolina's signers of the Declaration of Independence, and had married on Septima's 16th birthday, October 15, 1799. In 1816, they and their five children moved to Chilhowee, on the frontier, along the Elk River in Franklin County, Tennessee. They made their home on a portion of Henry's father's Revolutionary War land grant of 73,000 acres. By 1820, they had also built Rose Hill, where they entertained such guests as Andrew and Rachel Jackson, James K. and Sarah Childress Polk, and Sam Houston. The Marquis de Lafayette was their guest in 1825. Rose Hill was similar to Septima's family home, Middleton Place, near Charleston, South Carolina. It had a large central two-story structure, with two two-story connectors flanking two-story pavilions. Terraced gardens descended the hill toward the river.

Henry's and Septima's youngest son, Arthur Middleton Rutledge, managed the family property at Chilhowee. When Episcopal Bishop James Hervey Otey called for the establishment of an Episcopal school patterned after Oxford University, Arthur donated 410 acres in 1857 for this purpose. The University of the South, also called Sewanee, grew up on that land, with 10,000 acres in all by the time it opened. Arthur formed Rutledge's Artillery Regiment on July 4, 1861, in Morgan Park in north Nashville. Following the war, he lived at Sewanee.

At the end of the Civil War, a fire destroyed Rose Hill except for one of the wings, which still stands at the rear of 101 Lea Avenue. Henry died in 1844 and Septima in 1865. The house is seen here in a border engraving to the 1832 J. P. Ayres map of Nashville. The medical school of the University of Nashville is partly blocking the view of the house. A new structure was added to what is now the front in the late 1860s. Its most recent use was as a law office.

Across the street was the home of Thomas Green Ryman, owner of the Nashville and Cairo Packet Company of riverboats. He built his

Go around to the back to see the Rutledge home wing that survives.

The left image shows the addition made after the Civil War. The top right image is the wing that has survived. The bottom right print shows Rose Hill behind the Medical School of the University of Nashville.

home in 1885, facing Second Avenue South at the south end of that block. Ryman wanted trees planted on the rocky hill. To do so, dynamite was set off to open holes for dirt to be put into, and then the trees were planted. The north end of the block had the William Morrow home, which faced Peabody Street. Morrow & Company ran the Tennessee Wagon Works and were lessees of the work crews at the Tennessee State Penitentiary. Cornell, Morrow & Co. were wholesale dry goods and boot and shoe merchants at 68 South Market Street. In the 1980s I was on a Historic Nashville, Inc. committee that oversaw an archaeological dig at the site of the Ryman outhouse and Rutledge and Ryman well. Many artifacts were recovered and are now in the Tennessee State Museum.

THIS USED TO BE: The Rutledge home called Rose Hill

NOW IT'S: The portion that remains is for sale. It was recently a law office.

LOCATION: 101 Lea Ave.

Elm Street Methodist Church

Built around 1860, this is the lone Italianate-style church surviving in Nashville. It once had a tall, tapering steeple, but the top was lost soon after the Civil War in a storm, and its bell chamber and base were lost in 1925 to another storm. Riverboat entrepreneur Thomas Green Ryman was a member of this congregation. At the turn of the 20th century the largest Sunday School class in Nashville was here. The membership once numbered 1,200, but by 1971 it had become so small that the denomination closed it. The building retains its arched windows and doors and its cornice. In 1995 Tuck-Hinton Architecture & Design moved into the building and remodeled it. Earlier a telemarketing firm had used the building and commissioned Myles Maillie to paint two very large canvases depicting a church choir. These were hung on either side of the front wall where a choir probably had been at one time. Those paintings are now at the Tennessee State Museum. Presently Bob Dylan is working on converting the church of teetotaler Ryman into Heaven's Door Distillery & Center for the Arts.

This area was once one of the city's elite neighborhoods Professors with the University of Nashville lived near the school, and several churches were built here as a result. Elm Street Methodist, the Episcopal Holy Trinity Church, Lindsley Avenue Church of Christ, and several other smaller groups built in the area. Montgomery Bell Academy was built to the rear of the University of Nashville and operated from there into the 20th century. Academy Place

THIS USED TO BE: Elm Street Methodist Church

NOW IT'S: Future home of Heaven's Door Distillery & Center for the Arts

LOCATION: 614 5th Ave. S. (Rep. John Lewis Way)

The home church of steamboat line owner Thomas Ryman, this is now to be the home to Bob Dylan's Heaven's Door Distillery and Center for the Arts.

condominiums now occupies that site. The last horse-company fire hall built in Nashville, the Geddes Fire Hall, stands on Second Avenue opposite the Howard School. Beside it stands the Litterer Laboratory of Vanderbilt University. It is now a private academy, but the operating theater is still in the middle of the building. As Vanderbilt's medical department, Peabody College, and Montgomery Bell Academy all left, the neighborhood rapidly declined. Ryman's and the Morrows' homes were leveled, and a trailer park went up on the site. The University of Nashville medical school building was demolished, and Howell Park was put in place on the block. It is now the site of Bode, a short-term rental place. Many changes for the worse have happened in this area, but it is now on the way back up.

University of Nashville Literary Department

Built in 1853-54 by Adolphus Heiman for the University of Nashville. This was the main academic building of the school. It cost $45,000 and nearly bankrupted the institution. Heiman's original plan called for flanking wings and a tall Gothic tower. During the Civil War the university was closed and the building confiscated for military hospital use. This building was part of Hospital No. 2 and had 300 beds. With the high mortality rate of medical care then, prior to the discovery of sterile surgery and germs, more people died at the hands of doctors than on the battlefield. There was a whole room here dedicated to "Dead Men's Effects."

The University of Nashville was the life's work of a father-and-son team. Philip Lindsley turned down the offer to head up Princeton University to come west and build up the failing university in Nashville. He succeeded, and his son, following in his shoes, built up a medical school there as well. The Dutch geologist Gerard Troost taught there and explored the state extensively to discover its mineral resources.

Just prior to the Civil War the school evolved into the Western Military Institute, and Bushrod Johnson, later a Confederate general, taught there. The future Confederate spy Sam Watkins was a student there. Watkins was hanged in Pulaski, Tennessee, for treason. In time the Peabody Trust granted funding to the university to make it into a teacher's college. In the early 20th century it moved to 21st

THIS USED TO BE: University of Nashville Literary Department

NOW IT'S: Metro Planning Commission offices

LOCATION: 800 2nd Ave. S.

Built in 1854 at the University of Nashville, the former Literary Department building now houses the Metro Planning Commission.

Avenue South, opposite Vanderbilt University. In 1979 it merged with Vanderbilt and the surviving building was renamed Lindsley Hall, in honor of the two distinguished father-and-son chancellors of the University of Nashville. The area nearby has been redeveloped into additional Metropolitan government offices. The old Galloway Memorial Hospital was never completed, and the city took it over. The originally planned north wing has been added, and an annex to the Howard School building was also constructed, along with a parking garage and an expanded Nashville Children's Theatre. The former Literary Department building is now the offices of the Metropolitan Planning Commission.

Go back behind the old Howard School building and see this 1850s Gothic Revival jewel.

St. Paul's AME Church

St. Paul's was Nashville's first African Methodist Episcopal Church organized in 1863 under Bishop Daniel Payne. Its founding took place in a city under military occupation; it was an attempt to form communities among the newly freed African Americans flocking into the city. The congregation did well, and in 1874 it built the back part of this large brick structure.

The square twin towers and imposing columns (now gone) were added to the front of the building in 1914. By 1953 the neighborhood was no longer African American, and the congregation moved to 3340 West Hamilton Avenue.

This once proud monument in the African American community suffered decades of neglect and then experienced a rebirth. In 1956 Green Brothers Seed Company Warehouse moved in. Its stay was short. In 1959-60 the building was vacant. Hermitage Plastics used it from 1961 to 1965. It sat vacant again from 1965 to 1968. In 1969 Hermitage Music Company moved here. From 1973 to 1980 it was vacant again. In 1980-81 Neal Door Company used it to store garage doors. Vacant again in 1982, it was Dick Richardson Fund Raising from 1983 to 1996. Everton Oglesby Askew Architects then moved in and renovated the building. They moved out in 2014, and it became the Bell Tower event space.

THIS USED TO BE: St. Paul's African Methodist Episcopal Church

NOW IT'S: The Bell Tower event space

LOCATION: 400 4th Ave. S.

St. Paul's AME Church is now the Bell Tower event space.

Silver Dollar Saloon

One of the most distinctive buildings on Second Avenue is the Silver Dollar Saloon. Designed by Swiss American architect Julian G. Zwicker in 1893, it catered to the riverboat men coming up from the wharf at the foot of Broadway. It has silver dollars in the floor of what was formerly the ground-floor barroom. V. E. (Manny) Schwab purchased this lot and had this structure built as a saloon. Schwab went into business with his sister-in-law's husband, George A. Dickel. George A. Dickel & Co. advertised wines, liquors, cigars, etc., and operated from Second Avenue North and Church Street. From 1891 to 1901 W. W. Parminter owned the building. He was also a steamboat captain, so crews hung out at his bar. Three other owners operated it between 1901 and 1910. Photographs from this period show signs advertising "Hot Meals from 9 to 2," lodging for a quarter, and the local Gerst beer for sale. With Prohibition passing in Tennessee in 1909, saloons began to shut down. In 1910 David Egan opened the building as a soft drink emporium.

There is an octagonal tower near the street corner, and a pair of round windows with laurel wreaths around them on the Broadway side. There is a door on that side of the building, as well as one at the corner. Zwicker loved to use terra-cotta, so the trim around the doors is made of it, as are cockleshells above windows on both façades, an ornamental cornice, and wreaths surrounding porthole windows at the top of the tower. Zwicker also designed Brandon Printing Company up at the top of the hill on Second Avenue North, and Hundred Oaks Castle in Winchester, Tennessee.

THIS USED TO BE: Silver Dollar Saloon

NOW IT'S: Hard Rock Café gift shop

LOCATION: 100 2nd Ave. S.

Once a riverboat crew hangout, the old Silver Dollar Saloon is now the gift shop for the Hard Rock Café next door.

In the 1980s the Metropolitan Historical Commission had offices in the building in an attempt to promote the saving of the street from demolition for high-rises. The commission moved out, and Historic Nashville, Inc., a private preservation advocacy group, then moved in and had its offices there, along with a preservation bookstore on the ground floor. With the preservation of the street moving ahead, the Hard Rock Café moved into the nearby Watkins Block Building segment closest to the Silver Dollar Saloon and converted the saloon into its gift shop.

T. M. DeMoss & Sons

T. M. DeMoss & Sons occupied this building in 1938 as food brokers and remained until the street changed to retail outlets. The building dates to 1875. Until it was renovated for offices, the building had a hydraulic, or water-powered, elevator. To go up, you turned on a faucet, and a large drum would fill with water that would push a piston rod and lift the cage. When you wished to come down, the plug was removed, and as the water drained you descended. It was fun to ride in it, and definitely unique. Another feature of this building is its central roof skylight. Most of the buildings here in the warehouse rows had these to bring in daylight and decrease the need for gas lighting in the storage areas. This building is now flanked by a 1994 structure, the Wildhorse Saloon, and the 1924 Hooper Building. Owned by Gaylord Entertainment, the Wildhorse is a country-themed dancing, food, and liquor establishment.

Nashville's first commercial district, this street has housed businesses since its first store opened in 1786, up the street from where T. M. DeMoss & Sons would be. These businesses have evolved over time, from warehousing, distribution, and direct sales to business offices, retail stores, restaurants, and residences. Today you can live, work, dine, and enjoy music clubs on this street.

THIS USED TO BE: T. M. DeMoss & Sons

NOW IT'S: French's Shoes & Boots

LOCATION: 126 2nd Ave. N.

Going out "boot scootin'"? Get a pair here.

A water-powered elevator operated in the building until around 1980.

Charles Nelson & Company

Charles Nelson was born in 1835 in Hagenow, in northern Germany. At the age of 15, he and his family moved to America. His father sold his soap-and-candle factory for gold and sewed it all into his clothing. They booked passage on the *Helena Sloman* and sailed for their new home. A storm hit the ship, and nearly 180 passengers were swept overboard. With the weight of the gold Nelson's father was drowned. Nelson was now the head of the family, and they were penniless.

Nelson and his brother went into the family business of soap and candle making. Saving some money, they moved out to Cincinnati. There Nelson became a butcher and also took up distilling whiskey. Their next move was to Nashville.

Nelson opened a grocery in Nashville just before the Civil War. His most popular sales items were coffee, meat, and whiskey. Sales of whiskey outstripped the other products and supply was short, so he decided to buy the distillery that made the whiskey he sold. It was located in Greenbrier, Tennessee, just across the county line in Robertson County. In 1885 the company sold 380,000 gallons—or around two million bottles—of Nelson's Green Brier Tennessee Whiskey. Other well-known brands were producing less than 25,000 gallons annually. Whiskey from Nelson's distillery was sold as far away as the Philippines, Moscow, and Paris. Nelson was one of the first to sell whiskey in bottles rather than ceramic jugs.

Beginning in 1888, Charles Nelson & Company distributed spirits from Green Brier Distillery and also sold whiskeys and fruit brandies. In the back was Nelson's office, which was partitioned

THIS USED TO BE: Charles Nelson & Company

NOW IT'S: McFadden's Restaurant

LOCATION: 134-136 2nd Ave. N.

The number-one Tennessee whiskey prior to Prohibition in 1909 was marketed and sold from here.

off with stained glass and had oak paneling and a finely carved mantelpiece. Evidently, some entertaining was done in here for sophisticated whiskey sampling. Nelson's safe was still there as recently as 1977. Before state Prohibition in 1909, the whiskey he made was outselling Jack Daniel's and George Dickel.

In 2006 Bill Nelson invited his two sons, Charles and Andrew, to visit Green Brier with him. There they found the old grain house and barrel warehouse were still standing, and the spring was still flowing. These great-great-great-grandsons decided to revive the brand, so it is now available once again. Tennessee whiskey uses a charcoal-based process, filtering the whiskey through a mellowing bed of sugar maple charcoal.

The original home to Charles Nelson's Green Brier Whiskey. This whiskey *far* outsold Jack Daniel's and George Dickel whiskey. Nelson was an innovator in the use of glass bottles to sell liquor.

Cheek-Neal Coffee Company

Founded in 1892 by Joel Owsley Cheek and John W. Neal in Nashville, the Cheek-Neal Coffee Company, the originators of Maxwell House Coffee, worked from this location beginning in 1901. In 1907 Theodore Roosevelt visited Nashville, and while visiting Andrew Jackson's home, the Hermitage, he was served a cup of Maxwell House coffee. He proclaimed it "good to the last drop!" and a motto was born. Cheek-Neal first used it in their marketing in 1917. It was attested to by a man who would become president of the Tennessee Historical Society, and the Theodore Roosevelt Association also attested to the story being true. The company was acquired by Postum Cereal Company in 1928 for nearly $40 million. The next year the company re-branded as General Foods.

Leslie Cheek, Joel Cheek's cousin, had invested in Maxwell House stock. When Postum purchased the coffee brand, Leslie reinvested his earnings in a new start-up company called International Business Machines, IBM. He did very well with the stock. Nashville Sash and Door also occupied this building and had been in various locations selling these products since the 1840s. Second Avenue was revitalized beginning in the 1970s and 1980s and is now oriented toward retail, office, condominium, and entertainment spaces.

Rare Foreign and More bookstore was in the building in the 1980s and was a fun place to look at old and used books, meet up with friends, and then grab a bite to eat across the street at Laurel's, which used to be

THIS USED TO BE: Cheek-Neal Coffee Company

NOW IT'S: B. B. King's Blues Club

LOCATION: 148–152 2nd Ave. N.

Maxwell House Coffee's home office until General Foods bought them out in the early 20th century.

there. It had delicious gumbo, which I enjoyed on cold days. B. B. King's Blues Club & Restaurant is in a portion of this building now. Come on in for good food, good company, and great music.

Maxwell House Coffee is "good to the last drop." President Theodore Roosevelt is credited with this saying about Nashville's famous coffee.

Spring Brook Building

This is the oldest intact building on the street. Built in 1869, it has housed McCrea & Co. (cotton and tobacco brokers and commission merchants) and the Orr Brothers (wholesale grocers and liquor merchants). In 1870 the building was described as being "elaborately ornamented and beautiful, rich and costly in their designs." It reportedly cost $140,000 to build.

In 1981 one of the first restaurants to open on Second Avenue was the Old Spaghetti Factory. It was an immediate hit. Decorated with salvaged architectural elements and antiques and with a faux streetcar to dine in, it was fun and affordable. It lasted until Christmas Day of 2020, when a bomber blew himself up and severely damaged over 60 buildings along Second Avenue. The buildings on Second between Church Street and Commerce Street took the brunt of the impact from the blast, and they are still being renovated. Among these buildings were the Coyote Ugly Saloon, Buffalo Billiards, Dick's Last Resort, the Studio 154 Luxury Hotel, and the Lofts at 160. The landlord of the Spring Brook Building announced that they would not renew the 40-year lease on the property, and the Old Spaghetti Factory is now closed.

THIS USED TO BE: McCrea & Co. cotton and tobacco brokers

NOW IT'S: Vacant

LOCATION: 154-162 2nd Ave. N.

This is the oldest building still standing on Second Avenue North.

Badly damaged by a bomb on Christmas Day 2020, the building is being repaired.

C. T. Cheek & Son

Erected in 1898 and occupied by C. T. Cheek & Son in 1901, this structure was where Leslie Cheek, the son and partner in the firm, began work in the wholesale grocery business. He later sold his Maxwell House Coffee stock to General Foods and invested in a new start-up company—IBM. With his new wealth, he built an estate in 1932 for his family, which they named Cheekwood. His wife's maiden name was Wood, so he put both family names together for the name of their new home. That home is now Cheekwood Estate & Gardens, with a fine arts collection, extensive formal and informal gardens, and a large sculpture trail through the woods.

At one point Murdock Mendelsohn & Co. sold retail display fixtures here. They began business in 1935. With the increase in entertainment and food service on the street, this business relocated to Dickerson Road.

Now the building is home to Hooters, which among other things is known for its fried pickles, chicken wings, curly fries, and hot wings. The "Hooters Girls" are famous for their attire. The Beer Seller is at the ground floor in the rear, with an extensive menu of beers.

Cheekwood Estate & Gardens is open to the public.

THIS USED TO BE: C. T. Cheek & Son

NOW IT'S: Hooters

LOCATION: 184 2nd Ave. N.

Once a wholesale grocers, now Hooters bar and restaurant.

George A. Dickel Company and Roberts Candy Company

George A. Dickel was born in 1818 in Germany and emigrated to America in 1844. He began a retail business in Nashville in the 1850s and went into the liquor trade in 1861. With 70,000 Federal troops occupying Nashville during the Civil War, this was a great time to be selling liquor. After the war he had a liquor store on South Third Avenue. In 1869, the George A. Dickel Co. was founded and rented property at 201-203 Second Avenue North. In 1882, the company created this building to be its distribution headquarters. Dickel bought whiskey from distillers in the region and sold it by the barrel, jug, and bottle. In 1871 Meier Salzkotter became a partner, as did Dickel's brother-in-law, Victor Emmanuel Shwab, in 1881

Whiskey was distilled at Cascade Hollow, near Normandy, Tennessee, using a local spring as the water source. John F. Brown and F. E. Cunningham were the distillers in the 1870s. Matthew Sims bought Brown's share in 1879, and McLin Davis joined them in 1883. Davis then became the distiller, and he came up with the recipe for Cascade. He said that his product was "Mellow as Moonlight," as he cooled the mash at night.

Following an accident in 1886 Dickel declined, and his brother-in-law, Shwab, took over the firm's operation. In 1888 Shwab bought out Sims's share in the firm. That made Dickel and Company the sole

THIS USED TO BE: George A. Dickel Co.

NOW IT'S: Rocket Fizz candy shop and Downtown Smoke Shop

LOCATION: 201-203 2nd Ave. N.

Built to house George Dickel's distribution offices, and then a candy store, it is once again a candy store.

distributor of Cascade. After statewide Prohibition was enacted in 1909, Dickel could no longer sell its product in Tennessee. In 1917, the property was sold, and the Roberts Candy Company purchased the site. The west side of Second Avenue had the façades removed from Broadway to Church Street in 1934 to accommodate freight trucks that were new to the warehousing businesses on the street. The street had been designed for horse-drawn wagons that did not have a wide turning radius. Dickel and Charles Nelson's Green Brier both had distribution warehouses on this street. Beginning in the late 1970s the street was reactivated into a vibrant area of shops, housing, dining, and entertainment. This building now has offices on the second and third floors, and two shops on the ground level. Following the Christmas Day bombing in 2020, the street is being reimagined once more, with plans for streetscaping, murals, and a retail passageway linking Second and First avenues, which will enliven the waterfront for more events and shopping.

Washington Manufacturing Company

The Morris & Stratton Building was up the street at 218–220. It was built in 1854. Unfortunately, the entire building was demolished, and only the façade was saved. Another tragic loss on this historic street took place in the mid-1980s. An out-of-state property developer wanted to demolish the whole block between Church and Bank Streets, but the city would not grant that request. Then the entire block caught fire one night and was a total loss. The fire marshal found the cause of the fire to be "Out of State."

R. W. Comer was a traveling salesman, born in Kentucky before the Civil War and moving to Nashville in the early 20th century. He founded a successful apparel company, Washington Manufacturing Company, which made work clothes under the brand name Dee Cee. At one point the company employed over 20,000 people in over two dozen factories across the South.

In 1946 Comer chartered a foundation into which he began to build up assets. A fervent member of the Church of Christ, he named it the Church of Christ Foundation, with the intent to fund denomination-specific charitable causes. The foundation owned the majority of the stock in Washington Manufacturing. This would ultimately lead to a power struggle.

The company did very well in the 1950s and 1960s selling its clothing line to small, rural independent apparel stores. With the rise of Kmart and Walmart, these stores were put out of business. The company did not work to cultivate these new retailers. Debts had been run up with acquisitions made in the 1950s and 1960s. R. W. Comer had retired in 1946 and given over the management of the firm to his son Wick Comer. Wick and the Church of Christ Foundation battled over who had ultimate control of the company. With its market

Check out the cast-iron pilasters, with a Federal Shield, and the 19th century street address on that shield.

Commerce began in Nashville along this street, then named Market Street. The first store opened in 1786. One of the stores here was Morris and Stratton, and its façade survives at 218–220. It served as a hospital during the Civil War.

drying up, large debts, and the fight for control, the company was sold in 1986 to Van Hill. He tried to sell off assets, failed at that, and in 1988 the company declared bankruptcy. Out-of-town developers purchased the row of buildings on Second Avenue and renovated them into offices.

THIS USED TO BE: Morris & Stratton Wholesale Grocers

NOW IT'S: New Western Mortgage Brokers

LOCATION: 218 2nd Ave. N.

Gray & Dudley Building

Gray & Dudley was formed around 1880 by John Gray and Robert Dudley, both well-known hardware retailers. In 1895 they sold shares in the company. By 1900 they were the largest hardware dealer in Middle Tennessee. They sold tools, utensils, toys, ornaments, fishing tackle, and guns and used a 1,200-page catalog to market their wares. Sears and Montgomery Ward were already well established in the catalog sales market, so Gray & Dudley dropped its catalog and switched over to producing what it sold. In 1904 the company opened a large iron foundry off of Charlotte and 23rd. Around 1907 it won a state contract to build a foundry in the State Penitentiary, Gray having been the mayor of Nashville from 1897 to 1899. The company made cast iron stoves, under the Washington brand name, and operated the foundry at the penitentiary until 1937. They paid the convicts less than half what they paid free laborers. Gray & Dudley sold their stoves widely and boasted that the sun never set on a Washington stove.

The Gray & Dudley Hardware Company Building was erected in 1900. The company sold hardware and boasted 25 salesmen on the road that year east of the Mississippi and south of the Ohio. The building is the only structure on the west side of Second Avenue to have imposing façades on both Second and Third avenues. Constructed of steel, pressed brick, and stone, it contained a retail department, a catalog department, business offices, a wholesale packing room, a sample room, a cutlery room, and four floors of storerooms.

Today the building is part of the 21c hotel chain. The boutique hotel has a restaurant as well as a rotating contemporary art collection

Robert Dudley's brother was Guilford Dudley, a founder of Life & Casualty Insurance Company. Guilford's wife, Anne Dallas Dudley, was the leader of the Tennessee Equal Suffrage Association in Tennessee.

Erected in 1900 as a hardware distributor showroom and warehouse, this building is now the 21c Hotel.

from around the world in its galleries, meeting rooms, and hallways in the elegant hotel. It is one of the largest multi-venue contemporary art museums in the country, with more than 10,500 square feet of curated exhibition space. The galleries are free and open to the public, with online virtual tours available. Gray & Dudley is a restaurant on the ground floor.

THIS USED TO BE: Gray & Dudley Hardware Co. Building

NOW IT'S: 21c Hotel

LOCATION: 225 2nd Ave. N.

Brandon Printing Company

Charles Brandon started his business in the 1870s, having previously worked for the Southern Methodist Publishing House. By 1900 the Brandon Printing Company was the largest printer in Nashville. It worked with religious publishers, as this was a very big business in town. It also printed official bank documents, such as deeds, stocks, and bonds. From this Second Avenue location the company ran the first office supply store in town, selling typewriters, stationery, desks, and chairs.

By 1900 the company had around 125 employees, but the Great Depression ended it. Washington Manufacturing bought the building and expanded its apparel factory into it.

Built in 1892, the Brandon Printing Company building was the work of architect Julian G. Zwicker, who also designed the Silver Dollar Saloon; Connell, Hall & McLester; and Hundred Oaks Castle in Winchester. In 1939, the Washington Manufacturing Company took over all the buildings on the block and continued to make Dee Cee jeans there until the 1980s. Notice Zwicker's wonderful use of terra-cotta on this building. A satyr head is on the capitals to the pilasters on the ground floor; a dragon with open wings is holding up the balcony at the top. This dragon is seen in a larger size across the river at the former Tulip Street United Methodist Church on Russell Street. Printing and publishing were big business in Nashville up into

THIS USED TO BE: Brandon Printing Company

NOW IT'S: Available for lease

LOCATION: 222 2nd Ave. N.

Nashville was once one of the country's leading publishing centers, serving as headquarters for many religious and commercial printers and publishers. This is one of the surviving buildings from that industry.

the 1980s. Brandon, Ambrose, Marshall & Bruce, McQuiddy, Baird Ward, and Williams were all big firms here for many years, along with religious publishing houses for the United Methodist, Southern Baptist, and National Baptist denominations. With the rise of digital media, the printing businesses have either closed or greatly downsized.

Davidson County Courthouse, Public Square

The Davidson County Courthouse originally occupied only the eastern third of the present building's site. Second Avenue, then known as Market Street, went right through where the doors are now. The western third of the site had a farmers market and later a city hall. F R. Hirons and Emmons H. Woolwine designed the present building in 1937 with a combination of classicism and Art Deco including murals in the lobby by nationally acclaimed artist Dean Cornwell. The murals depict an outline map of the city of Nashville in 1937 and an outline map of Davidson County. Superimposed over these maps are figures representing Agriculture with a female figure and Industry with a male blacksmith. For Nashville, Commerce is represented by a female figure and Statesmanship with a figure of Andrew Jackson. Trompe l'oeil medallions depict aspects of the city's history and famous personages, such as Kasper Mansker, the Battle of Nashville, Timothy Demonbreun, the signing of the Cumberland Compact, and many others. The electric ceiling fixture has signs of the zodiac in etched glass panels surrounding it. Several of the courtrooms have Art Deco paintings on the ceilings. On the frieze at the roofline are carved limestone heads of a cobra (symbolizing wisdom), a lion (symbolizing courage), and a bull (symbolizing strength). Above the front doors are etched and gilded glass panels of the Law Givers: Moses, Hammurabi, and King John I. Over the back door is a similar panel depicting Athena, which is appropriate in this "Athens of the South."

Go inside and look at the Dean Cornwell murals. Also go up into the tower on the east side of the park for the interpretive maps of the square. On the west side of the courthouse is a memorial to the civil-rights march on the courthouse.

Originally just a county office and the jail, since 1962 this has been the seat for the Metropolitan Government of Nashville and Davidson County. The jail is now across the street, and many courtrooms have also moved across the street into two new buildings.

The Public Square was tripled in size and then converted into an underground parking garage with a large surface-level public park in 2006. It has fountains, picnic tables and chairs, and a tower with images from photographs of the square over the past century and a half, which have been laser-cut onto stone display panels. There are maps showing how the square has developed over the years. There are also images from ads for merchants who used to be located on the square. In 1862, the square saw an army of conquest and occupation muster in to take control of the first Southern capital city to fall to the United States Army. The civil-rights marches to desegregate public lunch counters in Nashville ended on the courthouse steps, with Fisk and Tennessee State University students asking the mayor to call for an end to segregation in 1960. He did so. The city and county have consolidated government now, and so the courthouse is officially the Metro Courthouse.

THIS USED TO BE: A series of Davidson County courthouses and city halls

NOW IT'S: The present Metropolitan Nashville and Davidson County Courthouse and City Hall

LOCATION: Public Square

American National Bank/American Trust Building

Originally a four-story building with beautiful Ionic columns on both street façades, this building had 11 more stories added on top in 1926 by Henry Clossen Hibbs. In his 1947 book, *Inside U. S. A.*, John Gunther called Nashville a city of old money, all locked up in trust funds. This was one of the places where those trust funds were locked up.

The Seeing Eye Foundation began in this building on January 29, 1929. Morris Frank was from Nashville, and his guide dog Buddy was the first service dog for the visually impaired in America. Today this building is part of Hotel Indigo, which also occupies the Nashville Trust Building, designed by Asmus & Clark in 1925–26, next door at 315 Union Street. Being former bank buildings, some of the rooms have travertine floors, and there are still old US Post Office drop boxes in some of the hallways. Located near Printer's Alley, the lobby is printer-themed, and there is a speakeasy-inspired lounge featuring local artists and songwriters seven nights a week.

On April 26, 1916, Charles Trabue shot and killed Harry Stokes in Stokes's law office on the fourth floor of this building. The two lawyers had had bad blood between them for several years. Trabue had cursed and insulted Stokes in public, and in print in the newspaper over several court cases in which they represented opposite sides. Trabue had represented Stokes's wife in a divorce petition. She had warned Trabue not to put "any trust in Mr. Stokes." She further said that he was "the most dangerous, treacherous criminal living."

Trabue said that Stokes "had reflected on me repeatedly and with great deliberation. He had charged that I had sold my convictions. He had said those insulting remarks to me, and had taken them and had edited them and published them in the paper. I was not willing for the thing to go on as it was." Knowing that Stokes kept pistols in his desk drawer, Trabue went to see Stokes and to ask him to sign a retraction of the insults Stokes had lodged against him. Trabue claimed that Stokes

Originally part of "the Wall Street of the South," this building housed a bank. Now it is part of Hotel Indigo.

lunged at him and struck him, and that when that happened, he pulled out his gun and shot Stokes three times in the head. The trial lasted for several weeks, but the jury found Trabue innocent.

THIS USED TO BE: American National Bank and American Trust Building

NOW IT'S: Hotel Indigo

LOCATION: 235 3rd Ave. N.

Stahlman Building

Built in 1906–07 and designed by Edwin Carpenter and Walter Blair in a Classical Revival style, this building has a three-part plan of a base with columns, a middle, and a crowning top. Carpenter had studied at the École des Beaux-Arts in Paris and was one of the finest local architects. This team also designed Nashville's Hermitage Hotel on Sixth Avenue North, and Carpenter later designed many large apartment buildings on Park Avenue in New York City.

A three-story Doric colonnade forms the base, with seven floors of matching windows making up the shaft, and a two-story cornice. The cornice originally had lions' heads and anthemions, but the entire cornice has been removed. The first elevators in Nashville were installed here, with a total of six serving the occupants.

The Fourth National Bank originally occupied the lobby, with lawyers leasing offices on the upper floors. From 1971 to 2005 Metro government owned the building and used it for office space. It was then sold and converted into residential use.

Edward Bushrod Stahlman was born in Germany in 1843. He broke his leg as a boy and was lame for life. In 1853 his family emigrated to America. Stahlman became an engineer working for the L&N Railroad, and when John Hunt Morgan blew up the rail tunnel in Sumner County, a friend asked Stahlman to come south and to run the commissary. After the Civil War, Stahlman decided to stay in Nashville. He married and stayed with the railroad until 1880.

He twice in the 1880s helped to bail out the *Nashville Banner* from its indebtedness, and in 1885 he bought out the newspaper and became its sole owner. He expanded its coverage and set up a network of reporters around the state.

THIS USED TO BE: Stahlman Building

NOW IT'S: Stahlman Building Apartments

LOCATION: Third Avenue North at Union Street

The Fourth National Bank originally occupied the lobby, and lawyers used the upper floors. The first elevator in Nashville was installed here. The former bank is now a residential building.

In 1905, he and several other investors built the Stahlman Building for $750,000. A few years later he invested in the Hermitage Hotel.

Federal Reserve Bank of Atlanta

The Nashville Branch of the Federal Reserve Bank of Atlanta was designed by Ten Eyck Brown of Atlanta with the local architectural firm of Marr and Holman. Completed in 1922, the façade is unaltered and is a fine example of Classical Revival architecture. The massive portico with its paired Ionic columns gives a strong sense of this being a secure repository of the US Federal Reserve. Within a recessed entry are double bronze doors that lead into a two-story banking lobby. It has been altered with a dropped-in mezzanine now hiding the beautiful coffered ceiling, which can still be seen from the mezzanine. The marble floors and woodwork have survived.

One of the main reasons that the Federal Reserve opened a sub-branch in Nashville was Rogers E. Caldwell. He had grown up at Longview, his father's 1,500-acre estate on Franklin Road. Like his father, he had a strong entrepreneurial streak, and he started out working in his father's insurance company. Soon, though, he decided to go into the bonds market. Finding Northern investors not too interested in Southern bonds due to defaults during Reconstruction, he founded his own company, Caldwell & Company, in 1917. He specialized in small Tennessee town municipal bonds. He would buy them and sell them to banks—starting with his father's bank, Fourth and First National Bank. He used that money to take out ads in the *New York Times* and *Wall Street Journal*. He then purchased a securities firm, and thus acquired some of the city's wealthiest customers. With this new capital he opened the Bank of Tennessee. It existed only to hold the receipts from bond sales. Its motto was "We Bank on the South."

In 1924 a new headquarters at Fourth and Union was built. At that point the company had nine branches, including ones in St. Louis and New York.

Unfortunately, Caldwell's empire was a house of cards based on unsound accounting practices. Despite his wheeling and dealing, his businesses failed soon after the stock market crash in October 1929. In Kentucky, Caldwell was indicted too, by a federal grand jury. His friend and supporter Luke Lea was indicted too, and in Nashville

This branch was built to handle all the money rolling in from "The Wall Street of the South." Developers are looking to reimagine this Classical Revival bank building for another century.

impeachment proceedings were held regarding Governor Henry Horton's support of Caldwell and Lea. Caldwell himself was never convicted, but he lost his home. Lea served time in prison in North Carolina, and Horton was not convicted. The "Wall Street of the South" was no more.

THIS USED TO BE: US Federal Reserve Bank of Atlanta sub-branch

NOW IT'S: Vacant

LOCATION: 226 3rd Ave. N.

Bond Furniture Company

The E. M. Bond Furniture Company opened in 1902 and closed in 1916. A newspaper article in 1904 described the store as beautifully decorated, with music furnished by a Wurlitzer Orchestrion. "The first floor has on display a number of exquisite colonial mahogany suites, an especially attractive model being a design from the Martha Washington style. The display on each of the five floors is very invitingly arranged. The three model rooms on the second floor are furnished with the latest designs. The display of porch furniture in a variety of new pieces is unusually attractive." It was described in 1909 as "the house that has the goods and makes the low prices."

The company also had a fireproof furniture storage warehouse at Ewing and Wetmore. Originally, goods were delivered using horse-drawn wagons, but in 1904 the company announced that it had a "very large new furniture van for moving and employ[ed] only experienced, reliable men." In 1916 the company closed the store but continued to operate the storage warehouse. Percy Cohen Furniture was located across and down the street up into the 1980s. Lower Broadway also had many furniture stores in the second and third quarters of the 20th century.

This building has a long history as part of the furniture business in Nashville. It was vacant in 1918, but from 1920 to 1961, it was the Wherry Furniture Company. It sold radios and "Furniture of Beautiful Homes." Its motto: "Pay as You Use. Use as You Pay." From 1963 to 1972, it was the home to Payne Furniture. It then sat vacant from 1973 to 1981. From 1982 to 2020, it was home to multiple law firms.

THIS USED TO BE: E. M. Bond Furniture Company

NOW IT'S: Vacant

LOCATION: 211 3rd Ave. N.

E. M. BOND, FURNITURE CO.,
THE QUALITY STORE,
211 THIRD AVE. N.
NASHVILLE, TENN.

E. R. KROPP, MILWAUKEE

Opening in 1902, this was the location of one of the city's better furniture stores. It is currently available.

Check out the beautiful ornamentation on the façade.

Life & Casualty Building

Andrew Mizell Burton founded the Life & Casualty Insurance Company of Tennessee in 1902, which sold industrial insurance. Its first policy payout was to an African American woman on Jefferson Street. Burton sent the whole sales department there to deliver the $2.25 check, and they canvassed the neighborhood and brought back $7.50 in weekly payments.

Burton was a member of the Church of Christ, and this attracted other denomination members to do business with his company. He tended to also hire members of that denomination. He opened a men's and a separate women's apartment at Fifth and Commerce, across from the bus station, so that his employees could attend the Central Church of Christ that he led the efforts to build next door.

The Life and Casualty Tower (L&C Tower) was the first high-rise to be built in Nashville after World War II. It was designed by Edwin A. Keeble and erected between 1954 and 1957. When built, it was the tallest building in the entire Southeast.

Keeble described his design in this way:

"Every line in the Life and Casualty tower has a reason. Its tall, narrow shape provides light and a view. The [aluminum] fins protect it from the sun. The penthouse floors of boilers and air conditioning equipment were placed high to avoid extra rock excavation and the expense and bad appearance of a 400-foot smokestack. The ramp on the second floor eliminates the hill climb to the upper and main level of Church Street, splits lobby traffic, and increases rentable street frontage."

The neon letters of the L&C sign at the top of the building had a unique design feature that Keeble came up with. The sign alerted passersby to the weather forecast according to the color shown in the sign. Red letters meant rain or snow, blue letters meant clear and sunny, and pink meant a cloudy day ahead. The first day's forecast was for rain,

This was the tallest building in the entire Southeast when it was built.

This building was twice the height of any other building in town when it opened, and it was the tallest structure in the entire Southeast.

so the letters were red and appropriate music was piped out: "Button Up Your Overcoat" followed by "Stormy Weather."

Keeble's use of passive solar insulation was ahead of its time. Later, when he designed Hillsboro High School, he also used it on the overhangs on the stacked floors to screen the classrooms from the hot sun.

THIS USED TO BE: Life & Casualty Insurance Building

NOW IT'S: L&C office building

LOCATION: 401 Church St.

Third National Bank

Sam Fleming is the man who built up Third National Bank, through his savvy and connections with the city's elite. When Jack Massey needed funds to franchise Kentucky Fried Chicken and to launch the Hospital Corporation of America, Fleming was there to finance them.

Another leader who helped build up the bank and launch Nashville as "Music City," was Sam Hunt. Hank Williams once handed Hunt a bag of money, and Hunt asked, "How much money do you have there, Hank?" Williams answered back, "Hell, I don't know, Sam—you're the banker!"

Father of bluegrass music Bill Monroe was another Hunt client. For years Monroe had kept the money he made from shows in paper sacks under his bed. Hunt talked Monroe into opening a savings account at Third National. One day Monroe called and said that he needed some cash. When asked how much, he said, "About three sacks full."

Maybe the most important loan the bank ever made, though, was in 1946. Three WSM Radio station engineers were trying to start a sideline with a recording studio in the Tulane Hotel. They got the loan and launched Castle Recording, which would lead in time to the creation of many more studios in Nashville.

The front half of this building was erected in 1904, and it was the first high-rise in Nashville at 12 floors. The initial architects were Barnett, Haynes, and Barnett. It doubled in depth in 1936, and the lobby was updated in the Art Deco style. Independent Life, Third National Bank, the J. C. Bradford stock brokerage firm, and now a Courtyard by Marriott Hotel have occupied the building. Prior to the present building, the *Nashville American* newspaper stood here, with its

THIS USED TO BE: First National Bank, Third National Bank, J. C. Bradford

NOW IT'S: Courtyard by Marriott Hotel

LOCATION: 170 4th Ave. N.

This was the tallest building in town in 1904 at 12 stories. Now it is dwarfed by many others. It is now a Courtyard by Marriott Hotel.

back to an alley. The *Nashville Banner* was across the back alley, and later the *Tennessean* newspaper was in the former Southern Turf building. With three competing newspapers all using the same alley, and their employees frequenting the same nearby bars, the alley became known as Printer's Alley. It is still called that today, with a number of bars and restaurants lining it.

Check out the lobby and its beautiful marble.

Noel Hotel

Oscar Noel began his working life as what was called a drummer. Every Monday he got on either a riverboat or a train and set out to "drum up" business. He was in the flour business, and beginning in the late 19th century he and his brother Edwin built and ran the Noel Mill and Elevator Company and the American Mill Company. Flour was then Nashville's number-one export and earned it the name "the Milwaukee of the South."

The Cumberland Telephone & Telegraph Company was founded by James W. Braid and James Ross in 1877. They ran a line across Seventh Avenue to the home of first lady Sarah Polk and placed the first phone call in Nashville to her. James E. Caldwell, Rogers Caldwell's father, was looking to diversify his business investments. In 1889, he and Oscar Noel purchased Cumberland Telephone & Telegraph Company, and by 1900 the company dominated the phone business from New Orleans to Louisville, Knoxville, and Memphis. In 1911 they sold CTT to American Telephone and Telegraph.

It was this business background that earned Oscar Noel the financial backing to build this modern and beautifully designed first-class hotel.

Built in 1928–29 and designed by the local firm of Marr and Holman, the 231-room Noel Hotel has its original high-arched windows, chandeliers, brass railings, and marble floors and columns in the lobby. In 1973 the hotel was remodeled into Hamilton Bank, and more recently, it was converted back into a hotel. To the rear and across Printer's Alley is the original garage for the hotel.

The hotel has a rooftop lounge with beautiful views of the city and a marvelous view of the annual Fourth of July fireworks displays along the riverfront.

Opening in 1929, this was a hotel until 1973. It then became a bank and office building. Now it is a hotel again, with a slight change in the spelling of the name.

THIS USED TO BE: Noel Hotel, Hamilton Bank

NOW IT'S: Noelle Hotel

LOCATION: 200 4th Ave. N.

Utopia Hotel

The Utopia Hotel is now part of three structures tied together to form the Dream Hotel. Designed by Hugh Cathcart Thompson, the architect of the Ryman Auditorium, the façade is white limestone, with four Doric columns across the street level. The three levels above the street each have bay windows in the middle of each elevation. The fifth floor has four arched windows, and the sixth floor has plain rectangular ones. The pediment is pitched. Above the entrance is a carved band of acanthus leaves and a human face looking down at those below.

This area was known in the 1890s and early 1900s as the Men's Quarter. Bars, hotels, brothels, and cigar stores were big attractions in this block. It was so notorious that the fine Maxwell House Hotel, located across the street at Fourth and Church, had a separate "ladies' entrance" on Church Street. No proper lady would want to be seen on what then was named Cherry Street, in the Men's Quarter.

The Utopia was built by M. M. Gardner in 1884 and was managed by Ike Johnson, who ran it as the Johnson House. At one point it was run as the Bismarck Hotel, but for most of its very colorful history it was the Utopia. In 1898 a craps table and a pool table were in adjoining rooms.

In 1909 the *Tennessean* said, "The Utopia Hotel and Café has attained a reputation almost national in its scope during its existence of almost a quarter century. It has housed and fed some of the most noted men in the United States."

W. R. Polston remodeled the kitchen just prior to World War I, replacing all the ranges and utensils with the latest and most sanitary equipment. A new refrigerating system was installed in the storeroom

THIS USED TO BE: Utopia Hotel

NOW IT'S: Dream Hotel

LOCATION: 206 4th Ave. N.

The "Men's Quarter" at the end of the 19th century and early 20th century was an area no proper lady would be seen in.

with separate compartments for different articles in order to preserve their separate flavors. Charles Fellows was the chef.

In 1939 the building was sold to Cumberland Securities, and later still it became Nicholson Dry Cleaners.

Check out the excellent restaurant and bar.

Climax Saloon

The Climax Saloon—what more can I say? This was one of the main bars and brothels on Cherry Street in the 1890s. There was a large bar downstairs, "entertaining" rooms for gambling on the second floor, and a brothel on the third floor. There was a false wall on the third floor, with a narrow bench for the "girls" to hide out on during police raids. Built in 1887, it catered to a "certain crowd." With statewide Prohibition starting in 1909, Mayor Hilary Howse was asked whether he and the police protected bars. He responded, "Protect them? I do better than that, I patronize them." As mayor of Nashville for 21 of the 30 years of Prohibition, he certainly did. In 1889, 1891, 1894, 1897, 1902, and 1904 there were newspaper articles about gambling raids, shootings, and stabbings at the Climax Saloon. After it was closed as a bar, it was run as a billiards parlor until 1934. The Climax Saloon was owned by the George Dickel Company.

The second and third floors and cornice are clad in pressed metal. The ground level has square stone columns, with lions' heads about halfway up each one. These elements are all original. Unfortunately the building behind the façade was demolished to make the new hotel. Satyrs once lined some of the façade but were not returned after the demolition and remodeling.

In the 1920s, the Atlantic Life Insurance Company had offices here. The Chamber of Commerce's Free Legal Aid Bureau rented the building. In 1937 the US Fidelity and Guaranty Company worked from here. Louis J. Hartman Liquors brought back more of its true "flavor" from 1942 to 1961. From 1951 to 1966, Graphic Laboratories Lithographic Plates worked in the basement. Hartman opened the Rainbow Club restaurant in 1960. In 1967, Maxwell House Liquor Store opened, and it stayed until 1970. In that year, Embers restaurant opened on the Printer's Alley side of the building, and it stayed until the building was demolished. From 1978 to 1986 the Saucy Dog Hot Dog Shop was here. AJ Diner was there in 1990, and the Tennessee Banking Company and Petite Café for 1991–93. The Bakery Café was there in 1994, and Kebab & Gyros from 1995 to 2015. Nusha's Rice N Spice and TaeKao restaurants were there one year in 2005. In Pad Kao Thai restaurant shared the building with the gyros place.

The Climax Saloon was in this spot at the turn of the 19th and 20th centuries. It was a bar, bordello, and gambling establishment frequently raided by the police, so much so that the "girls" had a secret hiding room to evade the police. It is now part of the Dream Hotel.

From 2008 to 2015 Santorini Greek Restaurant shared the space. It was then acquired by developers to combine it and the Utopia Hotel into the new Dream Hotel. They demolished the Climax building and salvaged the façade.

THIS USED TO BE: Climax Saloon

NOW IT'S: Dream Hotel

LOCATION: 210 4th Ave. N.

The Southern Turf

Part of the notorious "Men's Quarter" from the late 1880s up until World War I, the Southern Turf had a bar at street level, and betting and a brothel in other parts of the building. With two newspapers located nearby, lawyers' offices also close at hand, and the Maxwell House Hotel across the street, a steady stream of men were always coming and going. Police enforcement was lax, and the mayor patronized these establishments. Men could get a shave, buy a new suit, have their hair cut, get a lunchtime meal, and have a drink or . . . "a nooner." The George Dickel Company owned the nearby Climax Saloon, a brothel, bar, and gambling establishment. Jack Daniel was reputed to have made the rounds of these establishments and bought rounds of his whiskey for everyone. The Southern Turf was the grandest in décor of all the bars on Cherry Street (now Fourth Avenue North).

A four-story brick structure built in 1895 and erected by Marcus Cartwright, the Southern Turf was operated by Ike Johnson. There are granite columns on the ground level, and a corner round tower. Originally the ground-level bar was mahogany, with bronze sculptures, mirrors, paintings, and potted tropical plants. After statewide Prohibition passed in 1909, the building continued to function as a bar, protected by the mayor and police. In 1914, it finally closed. Johnson had managed it for years and lived on the third floor of the building. He could not accept such a change and shot himself in his room. From 1914 to 1937 the *Nashville Tennessean* newspaper occupied the building.

Skull's Rainbow Room burlesque lounge and restaurant is now on the ground level on the alley. David "Skull" Schulman managed the

THIS USED TO BE: The Southern Turf

NOW IT'S: Law offices

LOCATION: 212 4th Ave. N.

Bar, gambling establishment, and now a burlesque hall on the alley side.

burlesque club for over 50 years. He was a beloved fixture in Printer's Alley, and he was often seen walking his toy poodles, wearing their rhinestone collars, up and down the alley. In 1998, 50 years after he opened the Rainbow Room, he was tragically robbed and murdered in the club. It did not reopen for 17 years. Now the building has a first-class restaurant, and the burlesque shows are back as well.

The Arcade

Arcades were first built in the early 19th century and continued to be built up into the early 20th century. They were the first enclosed shopping centers. Nashville's Arcade was designed in 1902–03 by Thompson, Gibel and Asmus, and local businessmen invested along with realtor Daniel C. Buntin to build it. An estimated 40,000 to 50,000 people visited it on its opening day.

The *Nashville American* rhapsodized over the opening of the Arcade. It said, "An immense throng of men and women were in attendance all day long . . . The rail lines coming into town offered discounts that day to encourage crowds for the opening.

"Besides the general decorations of the building, consisting of flags and bunting, the show windows of all the stores were arranged on an elaborate scale. In nearly all of them were real flowers and their displays were in keeping with the occasion.

"It has been the intention of the promoters of the Arcade to have the stores represent as many different lines as possible, and the result is one can obtain anything from a shave to a piano at the Arcade.

"In the balcony was a band, which dispensed lively music all day long.

"The Arcade building itself is an immense affair, being 360 feet long and 80 to 70 feet wide, this covering almost one acre of ground space. In the second story are offices . . . The large skylight above furnishes an abundance of light so that artificial lighting in the day is not necessary."

THIS USED TO BE: The Arcade

NOW IT'S: The Arcade

LOCATION: Between Fourth and Fifth avenues North

Opening in 1903, this was the city's first shopping center. Patterned after arcades in Europe, it is still a popular place for lunch.

The structure was declared to be the biggest draw to visit the city since the Tennessee Centennial Exposition in 1897, and it was declared to be the only one of its kind in the South.

It is a two-story structure with shops and restaurants on the ground level and offices, hair salons, and more shops on the balcony level. The contractor was the Edgefield and Nashville Manufacturing Company, and the Nashville Bridge Company installed the rolled steel bracing system. It is flooded with natural light during the day due to its iron and glass roof down the central passageway. It is a great place for a quick, affordable lunch. Just sold out of the original owners' families, we are waiting to see what its next chapter will be.

Morris Memorial Building

Built in 1924–25 for the National Baptist Convention, USA, the Morris Memorial Building was designed by the local architectural firm of McKissack and McKissack. It is a Classical Revival-style four-story structure, with Doric pilasters, triglyphs and guttae along the cornice, carved swags and torches beneath the upper cornice, and a balustrade at the roofline. The two main entrances have arched windows above the double doors. McKissack and McKissack is one of the nation's oldest continuously owned and operated African American architectural firms. It is now based in Washington, DC, and its projects have included the National Museum of African American History and Culture on the National Mall.

The Morris Memorial Building housed one of the first African American–owned banks in the country, the One Cent Savings Bank, founded in 1904. In addition, the National Baptists located their publishing in this building at one time. Richard H. Boyd wished to found a publishing house in Nashville. He knew James Frost, president of the Baptist Sunday School Board, and Frost took Boyd around town and introduced him to publishing firms in the city. He formed an independent, not denominationally owned publishing house. James Carroll Napier was one of the founders of the One Cent Savings Bank, which is now Citizens Savings Bank and Trust Company. He was educated at Wilberforce University and Oberlin

THIS USED TO BE: Morris Memorial Building

NOW IT'S: Vacant

LOCATION: 330 Charlotte Ave. (Dr. Martin Luther King Jr. Blvd.)

This building was originally the home to one of the first African American banks in the country and the headquarters for the National Baptist Publishing House.

College and graduated from the Howard University School of Law. He was appointed registrar of the US Treasury by President Theodore Roosevelt and served from 1911 to 1915. He was a delegate to four Republican National Conventions and was a trustee of Fisk, Howard, and Meharry universities.

This area has a long African American history. The Nashville Slave Market was across the street on the northwest corner, the African American segregated YMCA was on the southwest corner, and the Bijou Theatre was on Third Avenue. It had been built in 1850, designed by Adolphus Heiman, and had the largest stage this side of the Appalachians when it opened. Jenny Lind, "the Swedish Nightingale," had performed there to sold-out houses. As more African American businesses moved into the area the Bijou became a segregated theater for them. With the advent of "urban renewal," African American businesses were closed, and most of the area was demolished.

Ryman Auditorium

The Ryman Auditorium, originally the Union Gospel Tabernacle, was designed by Hugh Cathcart Thompson for Captain Thomas Green Ryman in 1892. At Ryman's funeral in 1904, evangelist Sam Jones called for the building to be renamed the Ryman Auditorium. Originally there was no balcony, and the curved pews surrounded a pulpit and a small platform. Preparing for the Tennessee Centennial Exposition in 1897, the United Confederate Veterans Association planned a meeting to be held in Nashville. The Confederate Gallery was then added to hold part of the anticipated turnout of 60,000 to 100,000 veterans. After the convention, the veterans donated funds to cover the cost of the new balcony. It was then the largest assembly hall in the South.

The stage was added in 1901 to allow the Metropolitan Opera to perform *The Barber of Seville*. This reduced the seating capacity to 3,500. In 1904, more work was done so that the French Opera Company of New Orleans could perform there. In 1906, dressing rooms and property storage space were added for a performance by Sarah Bernhardt as Camille. The Boston, Chicago, and New York symphony orchestras performed there, as did John Philip Sousa. Victor Herbert conducted his orchestra there in 1903. John McCormack, Ignacy Jan Paderewski, William Jennings Bryan, Carry Nation, Emma Calvé, Booker T. Washington, Helen Keller and Anne Sullivan, Anna Pavlova, Enrico Caruso, Billy Sunday, Maurice Evans, Katharine Cornell, the Barrymores, Helen Hayes, the Ballets Russes, the Ziegfeld Follies, Maude Adams, Marian Anderson, Arthur Rubinstein, Bob Hope, and Doris Day all stood on that stage. During most of that time Lula Naff booked the acts into the auditorium and kept all the proceeds in an old shoe box.

From 1943 to 1974, it was called the Mother Church of Country Music and staged the Grand Ole Opry. Its stage door and Tootsie's

The interior is open for tours as well as concerts. Both are highly recommended.

A revival hall when built in 1892, the Union Gospel Tabernacle is now known worldwide as the Ryman Auditorium. It has a rich and varied musical history, with everything from the New York Philharmonic and the Metropolitan Opera to the Grand Ole Opry taking its stage.

Orchid Lounge's back door were across an alley from each other. The performers and audience could have a drink together between shows at Friday and Saturday night performances. A new lobby, restaurant, and gift shop have been added to the rear, on Fourth Avenue North. That is now used as the main entrance. The Ryman is a National Historic Landmark.

THIS USED TO BE: Union Gospel Tabernacle

NOW IT'S: Ryman Auditorium

LOCATION: 116 5th Ave. N. (Rep. John Lewis Way)

Connell, Hall & McLester

Fifth Avenue was a street lined with shops at the beginning of the 20th century. The tallest building then was the Connell, Hall & McLester Department Store, which included the St. Cloud Corner (built 1869). The seven-and-one-half-story building was constructed in 1889–90 and, when completed, was the tallest building in Nashville. Built as the first large department store in the city, it closed in 1903. Shortly thereafter, the Cain-Sloan department store moved into the two corner buildings. The company later moved to a new building across Church Street, and in 1942 Harvey's Department Store opened. It eventually took up the whole north side of Church Street from Fifth to Sixth avenues and included some adjoining buildings on both of those cross streets.

The largest department store south of Cincinnati, Connell, Hall & McLester employed 150 people and offered a totally new way of selling on a large scale in Nashville. The Fifth Avenue entrance has a 30-foot arch, with the head of Columbia (America's symbol before Uncle Sam) in the keystone above the entrance. A tiled vestibule was lit by a large copper globe with 25 electric incandescent bulbs. The interior originally had a skylight and an open atrium going from the roof to the ground level, bringing in natural light. The Fifth Avenue plate-glass windows reached to the top of the arched entry. That sales floor was 60 feet wide and 170 feet long. A row of white columns supported this large sales floor. A restaurant was on the second floor providing local products, including Belle Meade butter.

THIS USED TO BE: Connell, Hall & McLester

NOW IT'S: Puckett's

LOCATION: 201 Church St. and 209 Fifth Ave. North (Rep. John Lewis Way)

When the taller of the two corner structures opened in 1890, it was the tallest building in town at seven and one-half stories. It was also the largest department store south of Cincinnati.

When Fred Harvey, who had worked at Marshall Field's in Chicago, came to town to open his new department store, he used the light shaft for the first escalator in town. When Glendale Park closed, he purchased the carousel and used one of its horses as the logo for his new store. A canopy over the sidewalk sheltered pedestrians along the street, and more of the carousel horses lined the top of the canopy.

Today Puckett's restaurant is in the corner of the property, and offices are upstairs.

Thompson Building

Built in 1868 in the Reconstruction period, this was a high emporium of fine linens, crystal, silver, and other fancy goods so loved by our Victorian ancestors. Charles Thompson would order from Europe and the East Coast, and his clients knew that they could expect the best from him. He was in business at another location beginning in 1845, and his son kept the business going until 1932. By 1900, Fifth Avenue North, between Church Street and Union Street, was well on its way to being the most fashionable shopping district in Nashville. Businesses had been moving west and south of the Public Square for some time.

The building originally featured elaborate architectural ornamentation with hooded windows, quoining on the corners of the building, and a sheet-metal cornice. Based on elements that survived along with photographic documentation, the façade was restored in the 1980s. The building had a restaurant on the ground floor prior to its restoration and now houses offices.

In 1937 Feldman's Fifth Avenue opened here selling "ladics' wearing apparel" and stayed in business at this location until 1969. In 1970 Music City USA Record Shop began in business. It closed the next year, and Revco Discount Drug was here from 1971 to 1977. The building was vacant in 1978. Good Life Cafeteria and Health Food

THIS USED TO BE: Thompson's

NOW IT'S: Jeff Roberts & Assoc. law firm, the Home Builders Association of Tennessee, and the Tennessee Road Builders Association

LOCATION: 213 5th Ave. N. (Rep. John Lewis Way)

Built in 1868 as a shop for linens, crystal, silver, and other fine household items, the Thompson Building now houses offices.

Store was there under different names from 1979 to 1985. Various law firms then moved in and out from 1987 to 2007, with one law firm still here, as well as several trade associations.

Skalowski Building

As Fifth Avenue North, between Church Street and Union Street, was becoming the most fashionable place to shop downtown, another change was happening. In 1908 statewide Prohibition was enacted. The saloons had to shut down, and other businesses needed to fill their buildings.

Ice cream parlors became popular. Two opened up on Fifth Avenue North. One was Ocean, at 231, owned by Pantellis Panagiotopolo from Memphis, Tennessee. The other one was Guth's, at 217 Fifth Avenue North. Maurice H. Skalowski was its proprietor. It was a favorite stop for shoppers young and old after they had visited one of the new moving picture shows nearby. The finest ice creams were served, along with sherbets and fountain drinks.

Built in 1908, this was a new home for Maurice Skalowski to operate his Ice Cream Parlor and Restaurant. The exterior is clad in white glazed brick, with four bays of one-over-one windows in each of the two upper floors. These windows all share a common stone windowsill. Above the third floor is a herringbone pattern of brickwork. The attic is highlighted with small, round windows that have stone keystones above them. The roofline is an arcade of rounded openings and corbelled brickwork.

The interior is intact on the second and third floors. These were the private dining rooms and a ballroom. These two floors are connected by a beautiful wide oak staircase illuminated by a skylight.

THIS USED TO BE: Skalowski's Ice Cream Parlor

NOW IT'S: Gobbell & Hayes Architects

LOCATION: 217 5th Ave. N. (Rep. John Lewis Way)

Once an ice-cream parlor and restaurant with a string orchestra and private dining rooms on the second level, this is now an architectural firm's offices.

The ground floor has been altered, but it still has its pressed tin ceiling. It once contained an onyx soda fountain, a Syrian tile fountain, and a musician's balcony at the rear.

The building was used as a Dollar General before its renovation and now contains the offices of Gobbell & Hayes Architects, who did the renovation work.

At 171 Third Avenue North, try the Legendairy Milkshake Bar if you need an ice-cream fix.

McClellan's

The Wilson Building was built in 1882. This block of Fifth Avenue North had a number of discount stores with lunch counters in them, and they became the focus of lunch-counter desegregation sit-ins in 1960. McClellan's was one of the first to be used in this peaceful protest strategy.

The *Tennessean* reported: "The Negroes were seated at the lunch counters. They were not talking. They were looking straight ahead. One or two were reading magazines. Behind them was an aisle which separates the counter from the hair net department.

"As the tension mounted, a group of white boys filed in behind the Negroes. Standing behind the Negroes with no policemen around, the whites harassed the students, kicking them, spitting on them, calling them vulgar names, and putting cigarettes out on their backs.

"A very old white man with a thin face walked down the aisle jostling against each Negro, then leaning against each and whispering, 'Black b - - -.'"

The African American students were arrested, and their white instigators escaped. On the first day, 150 students were arrested. Diane Nash was one of the Fisk University students arrested that day. She said that the smaller group on the second day was "a change in plans." She said, "We are stressing the moral issue. We do not want to hurt their business." As the demonstration started, every fourth seat or so was taken, to give whites a chance to sit if they wanted to eat their lunch. None did.

Now, this is the Rymer Gallery, a contemporary art space selling local, regional, and national artists' works.

Once one of the focal points for the civil rights–era lunch-counter sit-ins, the former McClellan's is now the Rymer Gallery.

THIS USED TO BE: McClellan's

NOW IT'S: Rymer Gallery

LOCATION: 229–233 5th Ave. N. (Rep. John Lewis Way)

S. H. Kress/ Kress Condominiums

The first S. H. Kress store to open was in Memphis, Tennessee, in 1896. The second opened in Nashville on March 20, 1897, at 420 Union Street. By 1918 the store had relocated to 237 Fifth Avenue North, which was becoming the five-and-dime center for Nashville. Woolworth's, McClellan's, and then Kress were there. W. T. Grant would open on Church Street, and they all had lunch counters, as did Walgreen's, Cain-Sloan, and Harvey's department stores nearby. With the money Samuel Kress made in the five-and-dime business, he became a great collector of Renaissance art. Bernard Berenson was his chief advisor on art purchases, and a world-class collection was put together. In the 1960s the collection was given to cities that had Kress stores. Nashville's portion is at Vanderbilt University.

An informal opening took place on February 17, 1936, in a newly built store at the Fifth Avenue location. Francis Craig and his orchestra performed from 3:00 to 5:00 in the afternoon and from 8:00 to 9:00 in the evening. The formal opening was held the next day. The newspapers described the store as being "almost as large and is built along the same lines as the newest New York stores. The façade of the building is Minnesota granite and terra-cotta. Inside the front doors are huge bronze door facings trimmed in imported Italian marble. The stair railings to the downstairs store are also of bronze." The ceilings on the main floor were 21 feet high, and downstairs they were 15 feet high. The main floor walls were cream-colored, and the ceiling was

THIS USED TO BE: S. H. Kress Five & Ten

NOW IT'S: Tinney Contemporary art gallery

LOCATION: 237–239 5th Ave. N. (Rep. John Lewis Way)

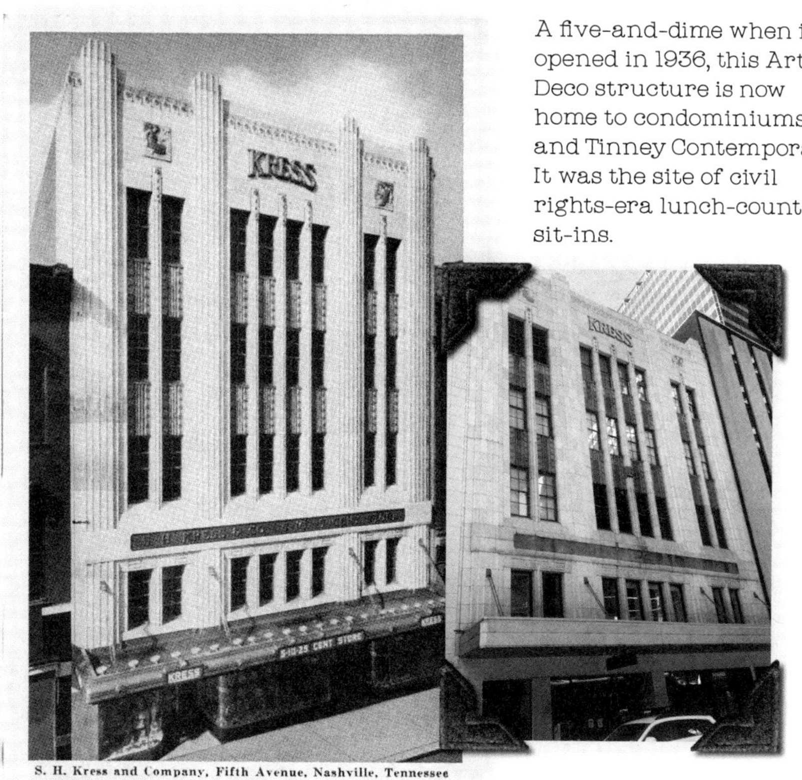

A five-and-dime when it opened in 1936, this Art Deco structure is now home to condominiums and Tinney Contemporary. It was the site of civil rights-era lunch-counter sit-ins.

ivory. The lower 10 feet of the walls on the main floor were trimmed in light brown zebra wood, satin wood, and French walnut of matched and contrasting grains. Today all of that is gone. The store employed 125 young women and 20 men. During the February and March 1960 lunch-counter sit-ins, Kress closed its counters and covered them up with merchandise. Woolworth's mezzanine counter is where future congressman John Lewis was arrested during the sit-ins.

The ground floor housed a McDonald's restaurant at one point, and is now the Tinney Contemporary art gallery. It is light-filled and always has a changing show by artists from across the region and country. The upper floors are condominiums. The original façade is intact and is a rare example of Art Deco in Nashville.

St. Mary of the Seven Sorrows

Built in 1845-47 as a replacement for Holy Rosary Cathedral on what is now Capitol Hill, St. Mary of the Seven Sorrows was described in the *Catholic Advocate* (now the *Tennessee Register*) as a "chaste and beautiful specimen of Grecian architecture. Its external dimensions are 110 feet in length by 60 feet in breadth. The ceiling is 32 feet above the floor, it is flat and tastefully decorated with moulding and square panel work. The front presents a neat half portico supported by two fine Ionic columns; and the entire exterior of the edifice is ornamented with pilasters placed at suitable distances, importing additional strength of the walls." Bishop Richard Pius Miles led the effort to build up the Catholic community across Tennessee, and when he died he was succeeded by Bishop James Whelan. His was a very difficult tenure, as the Civil War took place during his time. Fortunately though, he was able to complete the cathedral designed by Adolphus Heiman just before the war began. The church was seized following the Battle of Nashville and temporarily used as a hospital. Over the decades the church has survived yellow fever, the move of the cathedral to West End as the flock grew, the decline of the neighborhood, and its current revival.

St. Mary of the Seven Sorrows stands on the southeast corner of Fifth Avenue North (Rep. John Lewis Way) and Charlotte Avenue (Dr. Martin Luther King Jr. Boulevard). The first Roman Catholic cathedral in Tennessee, today it is a parish church. It has been substantially remodeled twice. Originally the tower had an open bell chamber with four clock faces alternating with four cruciform windows. The clocks were all removed. Double volutes were at the base of the tower and at the top. They have all been removed. A pediment was along each of the long sides of the building, and the windows had ornamental moldings and caps at their tops. These were removed in a 1926 remodeling by architects Asmus & Clark. They replaced the original brick and stucco columns on the front with carved limestone ones but the capitals are original. The original altar was replaced, along with the pews; frescoes on the front wall beside the altar; the original

This was the first Catholic cathedral for the whole state when it opened in 1847. It is now a small parish church.

gasoliers; and the ceiling, windows, and doors. Bishop Miles was buried beneath the altar, and his successors were to have been buried there as well. They were not, however, and his remains have been removed to the vestibule and placed in a large wooden container there.

Once the cathedral for Tennessee, St. Mary is a small parish church today, with a new, popular priest. It is the oldest church building downtown.

THIS USED TO BE: Catholic cathedral for the Diocese of Tennessee

NOW IT'S: Parish church

LOCATION: 330 5th Ave. N. (Rep. John Lewis Way)

Jensen, Herzer & Jeck

In the earliest years of the 20th century, Jensen, Herzer & Jeck were purveyors of watches, diamonds, china, ceramics, sculpture, and other beautiful things for the home. The storefront had large plate-glass display windows on Sixth Avenue, and the areas below these windows were black-veined marble, as were the two vertical ends of the façade. Above this street frontage was a large canopy to provide shelter from the sun and rain. The building had nine large electric light globes to provide illumination for nighttime shoppers at the windows. Above the display windows was a large leaded-glass window to bring more natural light into the store. A side staircase to the left of the entrance gave street access to the second floor.

Inside, the long walls to the sides were lined with glass display cases. The middle of that space had a large horseshoe-shaped glass display case for the watches and jewelry. All the cases had black-veined marble as their base. Modern electrical lights hung from the coffered ceiling and the center paneled column.

Later the building housed Dury's photography store, which had opened in 1882 as one of the first eight Kodak dealers chosen by George Eastman himself. The store later moved, and the business folded in 2020, after 138 years in business, because of the COVID pandemic. George Dury, the father of the photographer George Dury, was a Bavarian refugee who had been trained as a court artist to the Wittelsbachs, the rulers of Bavaria. He emigrated in 1849; his son followed with artistic aspirations of his own and worked in photography.

THIS USED TO BE: Jensen, Herzer & Jeck

NOW IT'S: Storage for the Hermitage Hotel

LOCATION: 219 6th Ave. N.

Diamonds, watches, china, ceramics, sculpture, and other beautiful things for the home were once sold here. It is now owned by the Hermitage Hotel.

This building, along with all the other buildings between the Capitol Boulevard Building and Church Street, is now owned by the Hermitage Hotel, which uses some of them for storage and rents out the others.

Tennessee State Capitol (page 188)

Tootsie's Orchid Lounge (page 14)

Ryman Auditorium (page 72)

at&t
ONE
WAY

First Presbyterian Church of Nashville (page 130)
Photo by John Guider

Union Station (page 150)

Belmont Mansion (page 170)
Photo by Ed Houk

AMERICA

Christ Church Episcopal Cathedral (page 146)

US Customs House (page 142)

Cross Keys Restaurant

The Chiles family owned and ran this Nashville restaurant, located in the Capitol Boulevard Building with entrances on both Capitol Boulevard and Sixth Avenue North. It was a well-loved family dining spot, eventually expanding to a second location in Green Hills Shopping Center by the early 1960s. It was run by John G. Chiles, who later served as vice president of business development at United American Bank and then as Republican minority leader in the Tennessee House of Representatives. With his increasing focus on his political career, the restaurant closed.

In the days before desegregation, the restaurant advertised for white women to serve food. Bus girls, along with dish rack and salad girls, were to be "colored, with health card." In food service all staff needed to have health cards.

Morris Zager's delicatessen was here in the 1970s and early '80s. Caesar's Italian Pizza & Restaurant now occupies the ground floor.

At the Anne Dallas Dudley Boulevard side of the building was one of the last locations for Juanita's, which moved there from its original location on Commerce Street, where it had been one of the city's first gay bars. Juanita Bruce Brazier had worked at the Jungle as a waitress. It was a place where straight men ate lunch during the day, and gay men hung out there at night. Juanita opened her own place next door in 1955. The bar was the subject of repeated police raids, during which the customers would be arrested. Juanita would follow the police downtown, bail out all of her customers, and march them back to her bar. One particularly rough period was when the police raided her place every time she bailed "her boys" out, and they came back and repeated that all night long. She finally went to the police chief and came to an understanding that if no "hanky-panky" was going on the police would not harass her customers. When Commerce Street was widened, she moved to Anne Dallas Dudley Boulevard.

This glazed terra-cotta building is a post-World War II infill office building, one of the few remaining from that period downtown.

One of the many segregated dining establishments downtown, this became a Jewish deli in the 1970s and is now Caesar's Italian Pizza & Restaurant.

Another tenant in the building was Douglas Henry Jr., a noted attorney and Tennessee statesman. He began his legal career as counsel to National Life & Accident Insurance Company. The longest-serving member of the Tennessee General Assembly, he served as the Senate finance chair for decades, helped to lead the efforts to restore the Tennessee State Capitol, and served as the chairman of the Capitol Commission.

THIS USED TO BE: Cross Keys Restaurant

NOW IT'S: Caesar's Italian Pizza & Restaurant, Page One Innovative Data Discovery

LOCATION: 221 6th Ave. N.

Hermitage Hotel

The Hermitage Hotel, at the northwest corner of Sixth and Union, opened in 1910. J. Edwin Carpenter was the architect. It is Beaux Arts in style and has a painted glass skylight in the marble-lined lobby with an entrance clad in Sienna marble. The Grille Room once featured the Francis Craig Orchestra, with Dinah Shore as their singer. Walnut from the Russian Caucasus Mountains panels the dining room. Unfortunately, the beautiful cornice was removed and sold. It had terra-cotta lions' heads.

When Gene Autry stayed at the hotel, he brought Champion, his horse, with him, and Champion had his own room. When the Tennessee General Assembly was debating the 19th (Women's Suffrage) Amendment to the Constitution, the groups lobbying for and against ratification both stayed at the hotel. The antis were in league with the liquor industry and plied the legislators with whiskey. This tactic swayed several votes, but in the end Tennessee cast the decisive vote for suffrage, and in 1920 women got to vote nationally for the first time.

William Gilbert Gaul, a painter of national reputation who worked in New York and Nashville, sold a set of Civil War-themed paintings to owner Robert R. Meyer, and they hung in the lobby of the hotel until the 1960s. Prints of the paintings were sold at the cigar stand in the back of the lobby. In 1911 William Howard Taft stayed at this hotel. Many other famous people have stayed at as well over the years, including Al Jolson, Duncan Hines, Minnesota Fats, Mitch Miller, Sgt. Alvin York, Woodrow Wilson, John F. Kennedy, Eddie Rickenbacker, and Elvis Presley. In 1980 the hotel used historic

THIS USED TO BE: Hermitage Hotel

NOW IT'S: Hermitage Hotel

LOCATION: 231 6th Ave. N.

A five-star hotel with a kitchen to match, this Beaux Arts jewel opened in 1910. Presidents have stayed here, and Dinah Shore sang with the Francis Craig Orchestra in the dining room.

preservation tax credits and was restored, with later renovations taking place in 1994–95, 2002–03, and 2021. It had been a run-down establishment in the 1970s, but like a phoenix it has been reborn as a five-star hotel, with one of the best dining rooms in town and some of the most beautiful interiors as well. The Men's Room downstairs is an Art Deco jewel, and women are allowed to see it provided that a male goes in and checks it out for them before they enter. This is a National Historic Landmark.

James Robertson Hotel

Designed by Marr and Holman architects in 1929, this building is 12 stories high and is in the Art Deco style. It originally rented rooms, suites, and apartments. The first two floors are clad in limestone, with limestone piers vertically banded, separated by plate-glass windows. The piers have a stepped-back top and foliated and geometric designs. The second floor has octagonal windows with more foliated detailing and the lobby has terrazzo floors, ornamental ironwork, a balcony bar, and a café. There is a fitness center downstairs off of the lobby.

In 1979 the hotel was sold and converted to housing for low-income and elderly residents. Forty-three percent of the residents were elderly, and 56 percent were persons with disabilities. Now it has returned to being a commercial hotel and was restored in 2017 to its original Art Deco beauty.

In 1930 the Pritchett-Thomas Company operated the hotel. It advertised it as "An Apartment Hotel of Distinction. Convenient to Churches, Theatres and Business District. Free Electricity for Cooking, Frigidaire and Lights. Apartments Furnished or Unfurnished. We are always pleased to show apartments. Home of Permanent And Transient Public." Jesse A. Pendergrass was the first manager. In 1937 Howard A. Gossett became the manager. In 1951 the hotel advertised "Single, Doubles, Parlor Suites, and Kitchenette. 100% air cooled, Basement Garage, and Friendly, Modern, Fireproof." Judge Frank Davis was then the manager.

THIS USED TO BE: James Robertson Hotel

NOW IT'S: Holston House hotel

LOCATION: 118 7th Ave. N.

An Art Deco delight, this opened in 1929 and served as housing for low-income and elderly residents beginning in 1979. It has recently been restored and is the Holston House hotel now.

YWCA

This was built in 1910, four years after the Young Women's Christian Association organized a chapter in Nashville. As the 20th century was dawning, young women were entering the workforce in offices, shops, and restaurants. The YWCA filled the need for a safe place for these single women to live and enjoy the company of similar women. It had rooms to rent, an auditorium, a library, a parlor, a gymnasium, and a pool and offered lectures along with classes in spelling, arithmetic, and public health. In 1978 the YWCA moved out into a new building on Woodmont Boulevard. This building sat empty for four years, but in 1982 it was purchased and the auditorium was demolished. An office tower was built to the rear, and the front of the building was beautifully renovated by Rutledge Hill Press as their offices.

It is in the Georgian Revival style, made up of red brick laid in Flemish bond. Limestone is used on the pedimented entrance surround, keystones above the windows on four of the six floors, and in a belt course above the first floor. There is a lovely inglenook beside the fireplace in the lobby.

THIS USED TO BE: YWCA

NOW IT'S: Dye, Van Mol & Lawrence Inc.

LOCATION: 209 7th Ave. N.

Y. W. C. A. Building,
Nashville, Tenn.

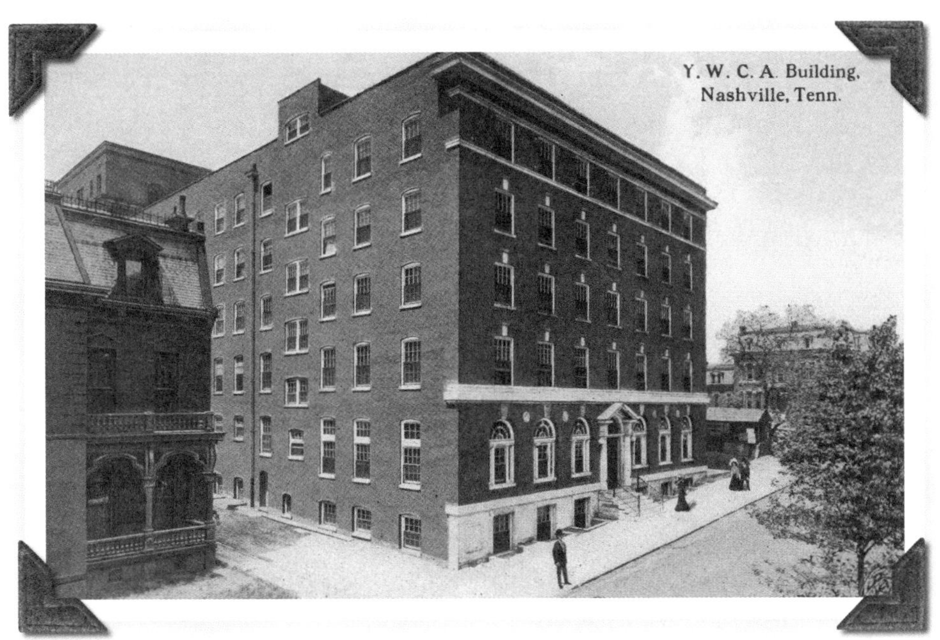

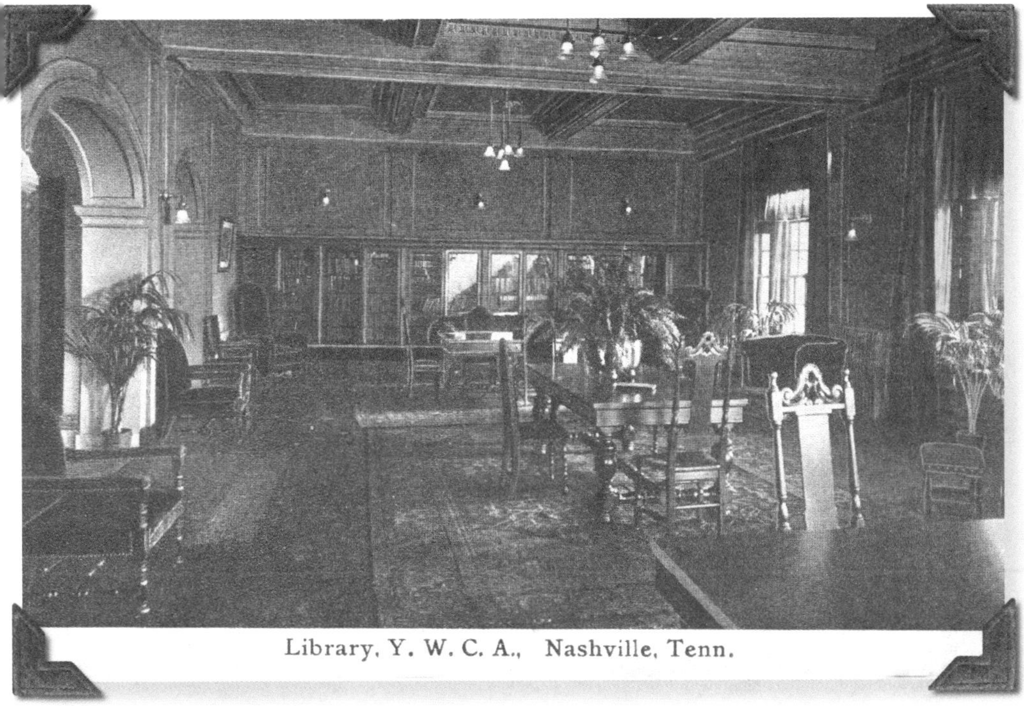
Library, Y. W. C. A., Nashville, Tenn.

Operating as the YWCA from 1910 to 1978, it later housed Rutledge Hill Press and now is home to Dye, Van Mol & Lawrence Inc., a PR firm.

National Life & Accident Insurance Company

National Life was the birthplace of the Grand Ole Opry, which started out as a radio show broadcast from the auditorium in its office building at Seventh Avenue North and Union Street. The audience originally consisted of clients who were given tickets to the performances. Being broadcast on a clear channel radio band, it could be heard in most of the Eastern United States, so it proved to be a great advertising tool for the company. The call letters for the station were WSM, which stood for the company motto: "We Shield Millions." After three moves, the show eventually wound up in the Ryman Auditorium from 1943 to 1974. Then it moved to a new home at the Opryland USA theme park.

As the company grew it needed more office space, so it purchased the rest of the block and demolished the Memorial Apartments, the Cumberland Lodge F&AM, and the Clarkston Hotel. Skidmore, Owings & Merrill (SOM) were the architects and engineers of its travertine-clad International-style building (completed in 1970) and the initial phase of the plaza off of Union Street in 1978. This initial phase left the former two buildings that had housed National Life still standing and a surface parking lot at Seventh and Charlotte. National Life had planned to build a twin tower at Seventh and Union and had demolished its original home in preparation for that construction

THIS USED TO BE: National Life & Accident Insurance Company

NOW IT'S: The William Snodgrass Tennessee Tower

LOCATION: 312 8th Ave. N. (Rosa Parks Blvd.)

Skidmore, Owings & Merrill designed this travertine-clad International-style structure to rival National Life's competitors' L&C Tower. It has been the William R. Snodgrass Tennessee Tower since 1994 and is a state office building.

when it was bought out by the American General Life & Accident Insurance Company in 1982. The Plaza was expanded over the corner of Seventh and Charlotte, and more offices and a parking garage were added below the Plaza decking. Relocating to Brentwood, American General sold the building in 1994, and the State of Tennessee purchased it as a new government office building.

Check out the plaza-level gardens for a great view of the Capitol.

Church of the Assumption

The Church of the Assumption is at the heart of old Germantown. It was built between 1857 and 1859. The north wall is constructed of bricks salvaged from Holy Rosary Cathedral on Capitol Hill, which was torn down in about 1858 as the Capitol grounds were expanded. The congregation was led by Fathers Ivo Schacht, John Vogel, and Emmeran Bliemel, the first German priests to minister to the German community growing up in North Nashville before the Civil War. Services were delivered in German until World War I. Across the street is the Buddeke House, at 1226 Seventh Avenue North. The church was organized in the parlor of this 1850s home. The rectory was built on the lot to the north of the church in 1874, and the school to the south in 1879. Several structural changes were made by Father Roessner in the early 1880s. He had new windows installed, a steeple replaced the belfry, and a new altar and reredos were added. Steam heat was added in 1895. In 1902 Father Japes completed the addition of transepts and a chancel and, in 1906, new oak floors, new oak pews, a large choir loft, and over 400 electric light bulbs outlining groin vaults were all added. In 1915 the parish purchased the Buddeke House across the street. Father Eichenseer asked Bishop Byrne for permission to have the area at the front of the sanctuary frescoed in 1916, and it was done. With America's entry into World War I in 1917, being pro-German became cause for concern. The congregation stopped holding their services in the German language. With the advent of cars, people began to move away. This led to a decline in the neighborhood that continued into the 1970s. The area then began a slow rebirth with the Germantown Festival organized by the Church of the Assumption and Monroe Street United Methodist Church across Monroe Street. Today it is a very diverse and vibrant area, with much construction going on.

One of the members of this church was named to the Roman Curia by Pope Pius XII. Samuel Alphonsus Stritch was born three blocks from the church and went on to become the bishop of Toledo and Milwaukee, archbishop of Chicago, and cardinal.

A German Catholic congregation built this home parish for the neighborhood's German Catholic members in 1859. The parish is now a mix of many peoples, but the building still functions as a Catholic church. The steeple was lost in a tornado in 2020 and is being replaced.

The church style is Gothic Revival, with three lancet Gothic arched canopies above the three entrance doorways. The windows above are similarly Gothic. The rectory is to the right of the church, and the parish hall to the left. Above a smaller reredos and altar, the church once had frescoes. that were painted around 1917 by Theodore Brasch. Now the sanctuary has light bulbs lining the ribbing to the groin-vaulted ceiling, and a much larger reredos and altar. The neighborhood is no longer German, and the priest is now from India. The people have changed in the neighborhood, but it is now a more diverse and vibrant part of the city.

THIS USED TO BE: Church of the Assumption, a German Catholic congregation

NOW IT'S: Church of the Assumption, a multi-ethnic congregation

LOCATION: 1227 7th Ave. N.

Frost Building

Designed by Gardner and Seal architects in 1913, the Frost Building was named for Dr. J. M. Frost, the first executive director of the Southern Baptist Convention's Sunday School Board (now Lifeway Christian Resources). It is the only surviving part of a once-vast printing, publishing, and evangelizing center for the Southern Baptist Convention. The Nashville Yards project has leveled everything else. This is one of the city's best examples of Classical Revival architecture with two imposing Corinthian columns, flanked by a pair of Corinthian pilasters. A beautifully balustraded parapet crowns the roofline of the building. In 1993 Hart Freeland and Roberts architects renovated the building. The church has since sold the building, which now houses commercial offices.

James Marion Frost was an American Baptist preacher. He was born in Georgetown, Kentucky, in 1848 and died in Nashville in 1916. He had pastorates in Lexington and Covington, Kentucky; Staunton and Richmond, Virginia; and Selma, Alabama. In Nashville, he served at First Baptist for three years. Frost founded the Southern Baptist Convention's Baptist Sunday School Board in 1891 and ran it until his death. He was given an honorary LL.D. from his alma mater, Georgetown College, and from Baylor University. A staunch conservative, he wrote several books on religion.

Frost married Nannie Riley, a cousin of poet James Whitcomb Riley, and they had three sons, Howard, Marlon, and Marcellus, and a daughter, Margaret.

THIS USED TO BE: Frost Building, Southern Baptist Convention headquarters

NOW IT'S: Frost Building commercial office space

LOCATION: 161 8th Ave. N. (Rosa Parks Blvd.)

Built in 1913, this is all that remains of a once vast publishing and evangelizing center that took up several blocks here. It is now an office building.

His funeral was held at First Baptist Church, Nashville, and included as pallbearers Major Eugene Castner Lewis, an executive with the L&N Railroad, and Edward Bushrod Stahlman, the editor of the *Nashville Banner*. He is buried in historic Cave Hill Cemetery in Louisville, Kentucky.

The office of Dr. Frost was restored by Hart Freeland and Roberts in 1993, using their original plans.

Gleaves, Claiborne, Savage, Zerfoss House

Built in 1857, this is the last large townhouse still standing in downtown Nashville. William Gleaves built it, but he sold it two years later to Mary Claiborne. She ran it as a fine boarding house. Made of red brick, it has cast-iron window hoods and a bracketed cornice, and retains its original front door. It has beautifully detailed parlors on the first floor, with the one to the rear looking down at a courtyard with porches on two sides. The original plaster ornamentation remains, as do the mantels.

The Standard Club, a Jewish private social club, added a large party room to the rear of the building around 1895. In time Dr. William Giles Savage moved his medical offices into the home and his daughter, Dr. Kate Savage Zerfoss, followed her father's example and had her offices in the home as well. She was an eye doctor, and during World War II she came up with the idea one dark and rainy night that white lines along the outer edges of roads would help drivers to see them in poor lighting and weather conditions. Such lines are now ubiquitous thanks to Dr. Zerfoss.

In the 1980s and 1990s this was a bed-and-breakfast, and the Townhouse Tearoom was located in the house part of the structure. To the rear, the party room added by the Standard Club was a gay bar called the Gaslight. In 2005 the Smith family purchased the property; they made major renovations in 2006, the father moved upstairs, and he and his son opened the Standard.

THIS USED TO BE: Gleaves, Claiborne, Savage, Zerfoss House

NOW IT'S: The Standard

LOCATION: 167 8th Ave. N. (Rosa Parks Blvd.)

The last grand pre-Civil War townhouse in downtown Nashville, it was completed in 1859. It has been a boarding house, a private Jewish club, a gay bar, and a B&B. Now it is a private conservative political club and public restaurant. It is to the far left in this view, which also shows Ward Seminary.

Ward Seminary was next door. In 1865 William E. Ward and Eliza Hudson Ward, his wife, opened their private school for young ladies in Nashville. In 1870 the Educational Bureau in Washington, DC, declared Ward's to be among the top three schools for young women in the country. The Wards were devout Presbyterians, and every Sunday they would walk their students the three blocks to First Presbyterian Church in their school uniforms. They attracted the attention of young men and were referred to as "Ward's Ducks" as they marched by in single file.

Tennessee Manufacturing

Samuel Dold Morgan, "the merchant prince of Nashville," constructed this building as a cotton mill for his Tennessee Manufacturing Co. When it opened in 1871, it employed 202 female workers and 66 male workers. Morgan had owned a dry-goods store on the north side of the Public Square in the 1850s, and a furniture factory in North Georgia. He served as the chairman of the Capitol Building Commission during most of the construction of the Tennessee State Capitol. The factory was built with its long façade facing the Capitol and downtown Nashville. As Morgan had come to love architecture through his work on the Capitol, his factory had some architectural detailing not always seen in a purely functional factory. It had a pair of square towers at each corner, with mansard roofs. There were piers between the lines of arched windows and corbelling along the roofline. Additions were made to the complex of buildings as the mill prospered.

Meanwhile, Joe Werthan entered his family business in 1908. It was in the rag-picking business and scrap metal. The company collected and cleaned burlap bags and sold them to grain elevators and feed mills. Joe and his brother Morris transitioned the company into the manufacture and sale of new burlap and cotton bags. When Marathon Motor Works closed, they converted that facility into their bag factory.

In 1928 the Werthan Bag Co. purchased Tennessee Manufacturing. It made feed sacks, flour sacks, and bags for all manner of goods. The book and film *Driving Miss Daisy* was loosely based on the Werthan family. Joe Werthan owned Warioto Farm in Williamson County and there bred, raised, and trained three-gaited and five-gaited show horses. The family still owns the farm.

Rolf and Daughters restaurant is located in the south side of the building and is an excellent place to have dinner. Reservations are needed.

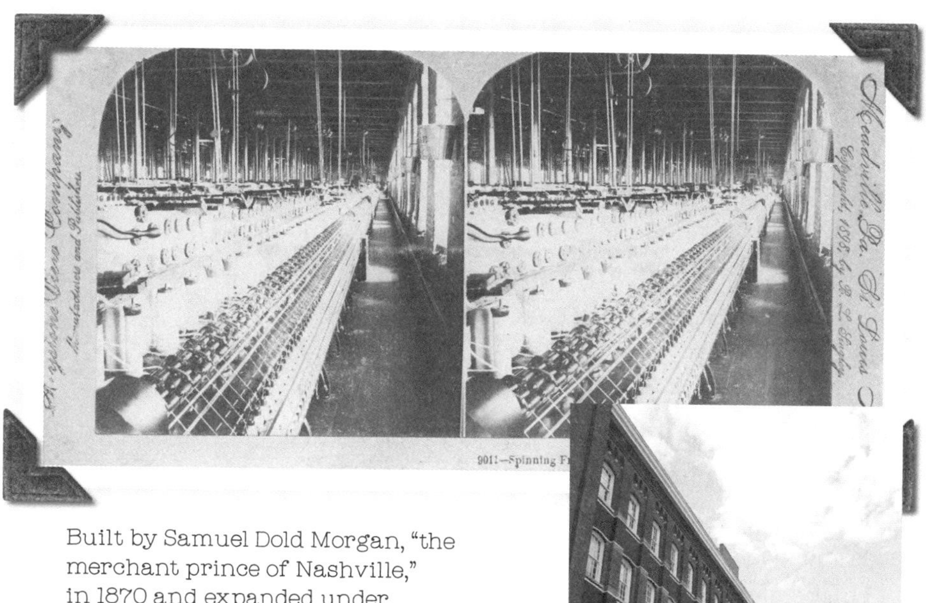

Built by Samuel Dold Morgan, "the merchant prince of Nashville," in 1870 and expanded under subsequent firms, it was a textile mill and a bag factory and now houses condominiums.

During World War II, Werthan purchased three properties on Elliston Place and ran them as the Werthan Service Center, a 250-bed facility for servicemen in town on leave. Funded by Werthan, it provided meals and recreation as well. An estimated one million troops were trained in Middle Tennessee. One of the largest and most important troop maneuvers was in preparation for the D-Day invasion of Normandy and the liberation of Europe. In 1998 the factory was sold, and the conversion to condominiums began. Five different phases followed in the award-winning rehabilitation, and new construction has been added to this revived industrial neighborhood.

THIS USED TO BE: Tennessee Manufacturing Company

NOW IT'S: Werthan Mill Lofts

LOCATION: 1400 8th Ave. N. (Rosa Parks Blvd.)

Printer's Alley

In the 1880s and 1890s places such as the Utopia Hotel, the Climax Saloon, and Southern Turf opened up onto what then was Cherry Street and now is Fourth Avenue North. The *Nashville Banner* and *Nashville American* newspapers both had back doors on this same alley, and the printers and newsboys all used it. With two newspapers, 10 print shops, and 13 publishers, this was a busy place. With the introduction of Prohibition, those bars closed on Fourth Avenue and reopened as speakeasies during the 1920s. Brown-bagging, where customers brought their own liquor with them, was overlooked in the popular clubs along the alley. With liquor by the drink approved by vote in 1968, it became a nightclub, dining, and burlesque zone. It had such clubs as Jimmy Hyde's Carousel Club (which Boots Randolph purchased in 1977 and ran as his own), which was a jazz club. Studio musicians would hang out there and jam after their studio sessions were over. Among them were Chet Atkins, Floyd Cramer, Bob Moore, Brenton Banks, Buddy Harman, and Hank Garland. The newspapers are gone now, but Printer's Alley remains. Today such places as Bourbon Street Blues and Boogie Bar, Alley Taps, Fleet Street Pub, Skull's Rainbow Room, Snitch, and Hidden Bar are in the alley. Such performers as Waylon Jennings, Dottie West, Hank Williams, Jimi Hendrix, Barbara Mandrell, and the Supremes have graced the stages here.

Skull's Rainbow Room goes back to 1948 and originally was a striptease club. It was recently totally renovated and has award-winning cuisine and live music, with some burlesque nights.

THIS USED TO BE: Printer's Alley

NOW IT'S: Printer's Alley

LOCATION: Between Church and Union Sts. and Third Ave. North and Fourth Ave. North

At the end of the 19th century, newspapers fronting on Cherry Street (now Fourth Avenue North) had delivery access on the back alley. Brothels, bars, pool halls, cigar stores, hotels, and restaurants gave this area the nickname "The Men's Quarter." The alley gave access to all of these places.

Bourbon Street Blues and Boogie Bar serves up Cajun cuisine and blues music. B. B. King and James Brown have performed on this stage.

If you are in the mood to sing, try Ms. Kelli's Karaoke Bar.

Nashville Banner Building

Long the mouthpiece of the white establishment, the *Nashville Banner* began in 1876 and promoted the interests of railroads and other special interests at the expense of workers and unions. The Stahlman family controlled it for most of its history. It was an evening paper and at one point printed as many as five editions (first, second, market final, sports final, and sunset final); these were later consolidated. It was in a good financial state during most of its history. In fact it helped the rival *Tennessean* to come out of bankruptcy, and the two papers operated out of one building, with one printing operation beginning in 1937. Editorial policy and news gathering were both independent, and this led to some newsroom cloak and dagger over reporters trying to scoop the other paper. The *Banner* had a pro-segregation policy.

Built as the printing plant and offices for the *Banner*, this is where a strike by the newsboys took place on July 28, 1899. Similar to the Broadway musical *Newsies*, the newsboys of the *Nashville Banner* went on strike when the newspaper raised the price the boys had to pay, but not the price the customers paid. The boys then refused to buy the papers for street sales to customers. They gathered at this building at the side door on Printer's Alley, where the papers were sold to the boys, and met there with A. J. Blair, vice president of the Trades and Labor Council. His son was one of the newsboys. An argument began between Blair and William Armstead, an employee of the paper's business office. Blows were exchanged. The police came and took both men to the police station and drove the boys away. The boys wanted to buy the newspaper at three for a nickel, and for the paper to take back what was not sold. The paper refused the boys' demands.

Look above the entrance, in the archway, and you can make out where the *Banner* name was in that space and was removed.

The evening newspaper, the *Nashville Banner*, operated here until the 1930s. The Captain's Table restaurant was in the basement off of Printer's Alley in the 1970s and '80s. It is now condominiums.

The basement of this building was the Captain's Table Supper Club in the 1970s and '80s. The club advertised Las Vegas shows, distinctive dining, and dancing. It opened on Printer's Alley on the south side of Church Street. Today the building is condominiums.

THIS USED TO BE: *Nashville Banner* newspaper building

NOW IT'S: Banner Building Condominiums

LOCATION: 309 Church St.

Cohen Building

Meyer Cohen built this in about 1890. Meyer's brother, Sol Cohen, owned "The Bucket of Blood" bar in "Black Bottom." It was a very rough place indeed. In 1897 Meyer married George Etta Brinkley, and they lived in this building. Their residence was on the second and third floors, with a pawn shop and jewelry store on the ground floor. The building had parquet floors, stained glass in some of the windows, and fireplaces in the rooms. The façade includes a recessed balcony on the front of the building, and that space was George Etta's room. The dining room was just past it on the right, and it had a large stained-glass window that is now in the Tennessee State Museum collection. Examples of original shared commercial and residential space are rare in downtowns today. This one has largely made it.

When Meyer Cohen died in 1915, both Peabody College and First Presbyterian Church asked Mrs. Cohen to bequeath her estate to them. Peabody was more persuasive, and she deeded this building and her collection to them in 1925. They built the Cohen Gallery on their campus. It was designed to be a fine arts gallery, with her collection being a highlight. George Etta had a life-estate living space upstairs until her death in 1930. The Church Street property had the United Methodist Church's Cokesbury Bookstore in it in the 1970s, and the upper floors were then hidden by an enormous awning with Cokesbury on it. It once had a custom-made military uniform store in the space, as well as a glass company, a sign company, and Ambrose

THIS USED TO BE: Cohen Building

NOW IT'S: Cohen Building Bridal Shop

LOCATION: 421 Church St.

Meyer Cohen ran a pawn shop and jewelry store on the ground floor and lived in the upper two floors of this building. It now houses a bridal shop and an Airbnb. Mrs. Cohen is waving from the balcony to her bedroom in the white brick building.

Printing. The top two floors were vacant from the 1950s on. Ty Osman and his two brothers bought the building in 2001; they gutted the interior and restored the exterior. Tony Giarratana bought it from the Osmans in 2012. It now has a bridal shop on the ground floor and nightly rental lofts upstairs.

First Presbyterian Church of Nashville

The first Presbyterian congregation in Nashville formed on the Public Square in 1814. It organized and formed First Presbyterian Church of Nashville, bought the property on the corner of Summer and Spring Streets (now Fifth and Church) in 1816, and put up a building there. When it burned in 1832, they rebuilt, but it burned again in 1848. At that time William Strickland, a founder of the first professional architects' society in America and nationally known for his building designs, was in town to design and supervise the construction of the Tennessee State Capitol building. An architectural competition was held, and Strickland was selected to design and build the new church. His design was far from traditional. He selected the Egyptian Revival style for the new building. It was the largest building in town aside from the Capitol, and a huge departure from the Greek and Gothic Revival and Italianate styles then popular. Today, it is a National Historic Landmark and the finest surviving example of Egyptian Revival architecture.

The interior has a vestibule with oak-grained doors and baseboards, a stenciled horizontal band on the wall, and huge double entrance doors. The sanctuary is the real jewel, though. As you enter, you pass through two pylon entries with vultures overhead. In the distance, the front of the sanctuary is frescoed and resembles the great hall of columns at Karnak. The eight matched windows depict the Egyptian desert and palm trees. Amun Ra is carved in painted plaster at the top of the cornice above the organ case and is painted above each of the pairs of doors flanking the platform at the front for the minister and choir. The ceiling is painted to simulate the desert sky, with clouds drifting overhead. Theo Knoch and John Schleicher, the same two German artists whom Strickland hired to fresco the Capitol, did this space as well. On the ceiling alone they used 16 colors simultaneously.

The organ has 2,100 pipes, with antiphonal and chimes. The northwest tower holds a two-ton bronze bell donated in 1867 by Adelicia Hayes Franklin Acklen, soon to add Cheatham to those names and the wealthiest woman in Tennessee. President Polk's widow sat two pews behind Adelicia, and Jacob McGavock, owner of Carnton Plantation outside of Franklin, was another member.

In 1955, after *Brown v. Board of Education* mandated the desegregation of schools nationally, a majority of the congregation voted to leave Nashville and relocate to the Cheek estate, in the segregated town of Oak Hill. About a third of the congregation wished to stay in place, but First Presbyterian wanted to sell the land for a parking garage site. The National Trust for Historic Preservation, upon learning of this, chose to hold its national meeting in Nashville and persuaded First Presbyterian to sell the building to its own members who wished to stay.

A must-see interior, this is a National Historic Landmark and the finest existing example of Egyptian Revival architecture anywhere. The building has stood since 1851. Two-thirds of the congregation moved to the segregated town of Oak Hill in 1954. The building now houses the Downtown Presbyterian Church.

Today the church fulfills Dr. James I. Vance's 1914 call to be a church not in some sylvan retreat, but to meet human need on the busy streets of the city, where it is clearly needed. A program to provide food to the homeless operates there, as does a clothing closet, and other community programs in the arts and music are featured as part of the mission of the church to reach out and help those in need. The *Contributor*, a street newspaper, with the largest such circulation in the country, operates out of the church, and it has helped hundreds of homeless individuals to move into housing. First Church has left Nashville, but good works go on at Fifth and Church.

THIS USED TO BE: First Presbyterian Church of Nashville

NOW IT'S: Downtown Presbyterian Church

LOCATION: 154 5th Ave. N. (Rep. John Lewis Way)

McKendree United Methodist Church

Methodism in Nashville began in 1787, when the Rev. Benjamin Ogden began to organize a fellowship here. By 1790, they had their first church building in the Public Square. They moved to Church Street in 1818, where the Noel Garage is now. Then in 1832, the congregation moved to the present location on Church Street and erected a new building. At one point, this congregation was the largest Methodist one in America. In 1845,President James K. Polk's funeral was held at McKendree. The Nashville Convention of Southern states was held in that building in 1850. Its purpose was to discuss the secession of the Southern states as advocated by John C. Calhoun. During the Civil War the church was seized and used as a hospital. The congregation grew too large for this structure; it was torn down in 1877, and another church was built on the same site. While it was being built, the First Presbyterian Church nearby allowed McKendree to share its building. In 1905 McKendree's building burned down. Construction of the present building began in 1906 and was completed in 1910. In that year the Von Guerthler Art Glass Company added stained-glass windows. The new church had twin open bell towers at the outer corners of the building and a dome in the center. A Sunday school building was connected to the rear of the sanctuary in 1932. The interior was altered in 1945 when the balcony was squared off and a central aisle put in place. In 1960 new pews, pulpit, communion table, organ screens, carpeting, and a chapel were added. Between 1966 and 1968 the latest changes

THIS USED TO BE: McKendree United Methodist Church

NOW IT'S: McKendree United Methodist Church

LOCATION: 523 Church St.

Home to the oldest congregation in Nashville, this is their fifth building. The front dates to 1968. Behind it is the 1905 building.

were made, with the façade being hidden behind an addition, which moved the church closer to Church Street. In 1990 the Christian Life Center was built adjoining the rear of the church and facing onto Commerce Street.

Look down the alley to the sides of the building and you can see the bases to the two original towers whose tops were removed for the large addition to the front..

Wilcox Building

In 1892, James Wilcox made an offer to buy the old Christ Church Episcopal Church located at the corner of Sixth Avenue North and Church Street. They closed on the sale that December for $24,000.

Wilcox announced that he would build a seven-story office building with two elevators and steam heat. It opened in 1894. The ground level was retail spaces taken by the Berlitz School of Languages, Fall's Tennessee Business College, the Royal Costume Company of New York, and the Tea Room restaurant. In 1895 Wilcox offered free office space to those in charge of planning the Tennessee Centennial Exposition.

In 1905 Major Edward Bushrod Stahlman purchased the building for $105,000. He planned to enlarge it, and move his newspaper, the *Nashville Banner*, there. However, he changed his mind and sold the building to John H. Hitchcock. The building then became known as the Hitchcock Building.

In 1911 plans were announced to remodel the west side into a confectionery store and ice cream parlor. John Decker and his son George traveled to other cities for new ideas on how to lay out their business. They came home and hired Marr and Holman to remodel their leased space. It opened in July 1911 and was a big success. The ice cream business was so successful, in fact, that they sold the store to concentrate on making ice cream at their plant at 1411 Church Street.

Liggett's Rexall Drug Store operated from that corner from 1921 to 1945. Then the entire block all along Church Street was purchased

THIS USED TO BE: Wilcox Building

NOW IT'S: Maddox Hotel

LOCATION: 526-530 Church St.

The Wilcox Building is now the Maddox Hotel and a Subway sandwich shop.

by Fred Harvey, and they were all connected together to form Harvey's Department Store. That closed in 1983, and offices occupied the building.

Today this is the Maddox Hotel, a seven-story red brick building with a Subway sandwich shop. On the fourth floors of both street elevations (on Sixth Avenue North and Church Street) are arched windows that originally had masonry balconies that have been removed.

Grab a quick sandwich here, and then go outside and check out the murals on the east and north sides of the building.

Castner-Knott Department Store

With the acceptance and growth of department stores, Charles Castner and William Knott opened their store in 1898, and did so well with it that they built this building and opened it in 1906. It had 10-by-12-foot plate-glass windows, canopies over the entrances, and coffered ceilings. In 1911 Castor-Knott added the Armstrong Building adjoining it on Church Street, at Anne Dallas Dudley Boulevard. Following World War II, the store was in strong competition with Cain-Sloan and Harvey's department stores down the street. So, in 1958–59 they hired Marr and Holman to modernize and connect the floors in their two buildings. A corner entrance at Anne Dallas Dudley Boulevard and Church Street was added, and black polished granite was installed around the large plate-glass street display windows. Unfortunately, in 1979 metal panels were installed over the façades to unify the buildings. In 1996 Castner-Knott gave up and sold the buildings. A 1998–99 renovation removed the metal panels, and the two façades were cleaned and restored. The buildings are now used as office spaces and Morton's steakhouse, an upscale chain, is located at street level, with a popular bar attached to it.

THIS USED TO BE: Castner-Knott Department Store

NOW IT'S: Offices

LOCATION: 616–618 Church St.

A department store from 1898 to 1996, Morton's steakhouse and offices now occupy the building.

Bennie Dillon Building

George Bennie and William Dillon were the two men behind the building of this structure. Bennie was the president of a wholesale merchandise company and had served as president of the Chamber of Commerce. His friend Dillon was a real-estate developer. When Bennie died in 1924, his family agreed to continue constructing this office tower.

This Asmus & Clark–designed building went up in 1925–27. Other buildings surviving by Asmus & Clark are the Masonic Grand Lodge of Tennessee, the Berger Building, and the Nashville Trust Building. Foster and Creighton were the local contractors. The Bennie Dillon Building is a 12-story steel and terra-cotta building, designed in accordance with the Louis Sullivan concept of the three-part structure: base, shaft, and cornice. The bottom two floors have limestone blocks and were restored following an earlier remodeling. Eleven identical floors make up the shaft portion, with an elaborate terra-cotta cornice at the top. Terra-cotta ribbons run up the sides to give the illusion of columns. Nashville's doctors were conveniently concentrated downtown next door at the six-story Doctor's Building, and with the expanding city's need for more doctors, this building was born. In 1998–99 it was converted into apartments, and it continues in that use today. The original marble lobby survives.

THIS USED TO BE: Bennie Dillon Building

NOW IT'S: Bennie Dillon Apartments and Condominiums

LOCATION: 700 Church St.

Originally the location for many of Nashville's doctors who wanted to have their offices in one central area downtown, this is now apartments and condominiums.

The Doctor's Building

Designed by Dougherty and Gardner in 1916 and doubled in height in 1921, this building was where the doctors of Nashville could concentrate their talents and clientele. It had been the site of Col. E. W. Cole's home, the last private residence on what had been a residential part of Church Street. Vanderbilt professor Dr. Matthew McGannon commissioned this Renaissance Revival confection, covered all over with exuberant glazed terra-cotta, lions' heads, swags, wreaths, garlands, urns, and two sets of cornices. Not knowing what a success he would have on his hands, McGannon built only a three-story building. Along that first cornice are terra-cotta shields based on the Medici family coat of arms. The Medici ran 15th-century Florence and even had a pope in the family. The family name is derived from the Italian word for doctor, *medico*. McGannon soon needed to double the building's height, but those three floors are clad in totally different glazed terra-cotta and have their own cornice at the top. There is a central light and ventilation atrium. The six-story building has 100,000 square feet.

Several hospitals moved to the west side of town in the 1960s and '70s, and doctors followed them. Losing tenants, the building was sold and converted by Tuck, Hinton, Everton Architects into modern offices in 1984–86. In 2007, with tourism exploding in Nashville, it became Homewood Suites by Hilton, a hotel. It now has glorious up-lighting on the terra-cotta at night.

Check out the stained glass in the elevator lobby.

THIS USED TO BE: The Doctor's Building

NOW IT'S: Homewood Suites by Hilton

LOCATION: 710 Church St.

Built as the first central location for doctors to have their offices, this building soon doubled in height, and then the Bennie Dillon Building was put up next door for the same purpose. Now a hotel, it has beautiful terra-cotta cladding.

US Customs House

Nashville was promised a Federal Building by an Act of Congress in 1856. A lot was purchased at Fourth and Church for this building. In 1870 Alfred B. Mullett, supervising architect for the US Treasury Department, realizing that the site and funding were now inadequate, traded the site for one at the corner of Seventh Avenue South and Broadway. By 1877 it was realized that this lot was also too small and that the 1856 appropriation was also too small. So the corner of Eighth and Broadway was also acquired, and the appropriation increased from $95,000 to $377,000.

William Appleton Potter designed this new building in 1876, and its cornerstone was laid in 1877 by President Rutherford B. Hayes. Hayes had stolen the presidential election by pledging to the Southern electors to remove federal troops from the South, turn his back on the African Americans who had recently won their freedom, and turn on the federal tap to spend money for construction in the South if they would support him against the wishes of Southern voters. It worked. One of his first acts was to come here and lay the cornerstone for this Federal Building.

It is a Gothic Revival gem, clad in Kentucky limestone with Missouri red granite columns at the central entrance. A tall Gothic tower with clocks in each of its four sides dominates the front of the building. Being at the top of the hill, the US Customs House also dominates Upper Broadway. Lancet Gothic window and door openings enliven the façade. Inside, the post office was on the first

THIS USED TO BE: US Customs House

NOW IT'S: US Bankruptcy Court and commercial office space

LOCATION: 701 Broadway

Built as political payback for the stealing of the 1876 presidential election, the US Customs House was opened in 1877. The Southern Electoral College members gave their votes to Rutherford B. Hayes—contrary to how their states had voted—and changed the outcome of the election. Hayes became president, Reconstruction ended, and money flowed south again from federal coffers. This building is now offices and courtrooms.

floor, customs offices were on the second floor, and federal courtrooms were on the third floor. A rear addition was added in 1903 and twin side wings in 1916.

When an annex to the 1949 Federal Building across Eighth Avenue South was built in 1974, the Customs House was declared surplus, and it was deeded to Metro. Gresham, Smith & Partners renovated the building at that time. It was again renovated in 1994 by Everton Oglesby Askew Architects. Ironically, the federal government now leases space in the building for a US Bankruptcy Court and once did for US Sixth Circuit Court judge Gilbert Merritt.

Hume-Fogg High School

William Hume and Francis B. Fogg were two early educators in Nashville. Two schools were built on this site in the mid-19th century and named in honor of these two men. Hume School was built in 1855 by Adolphus Heiman and was castellated Gothic in style. It stood on Eighth Avenue, toward the back of the present building. It was the first public school building in Nashville. Fogg School was erected in 1874 as the first separate high school in Nashville and second public school building in the city. It was built next door at the corner of Eighth and Broadway. Both were torn down to build the current school in 1911.

Hume-Fogg High School was designed in the Collegiate Gothic style made popular at Yale, Princeton, and Duke. Vanderbilt is now in a building frenzy in this style along West End Avenue. William B. Ittner and Robert Sharp built the central entrance and west wing in 1912 and completed the east wing in 1916. Above the front doors, carved into the stone brackets, are dwarfs holding academic symbols. The building has five floors, including the basement.

In 1942 the school was made into a technical and vocational school. That lasted until 1982. In that year, under a court-supervised desegregation order (26 years after the Supreme Court ordered segregation to end), it again changed course and became an academic magnet school. It celebrated its sesquicentennial during the 2004–2005 academic year.

The school offers 31 Advanced Placement courses. All academic courses are taught at the honors or AP level, except for P.E./art courses. Nearly 100 percent of graduates each year go on to four-year colleges, with many earning academic scholarships and grant funding from universities across the country. Each graduating class receives over $10 million in such aid each academic year.

Check out the corbels above the front door. They are dwarfs holding academic symbols.

Singers Dinah Shore, Phil Harris, and Pat Boone went to school here, as did movie director Delbert Mann and pin-up model Bettie Page.

In 2006-2007 the school received the National Siemens Award for one of the best science- and math-based academic programs in the country. *Newsweek* and *U.S. News & World Report* have consistently ranked Hume-Fogg among the top public high schools in America. Singers Dinah Shore, Phil Harris, and Pat Boone went to school here, as did movie director Delbert Mann and pin-up model Bettie Page.

THIS USED TO BE: Hume-Fogg High School

NOW IT'S: Hume-Fogg High School

LOCATION: 700 Broadway

Christ Church Episcopal Cathedral

The first Christ Church Episcopal was built on Church Street at present-day Sixth Avenue North in 1830–31. As the neighborhood transitioned from residential to commercial, the congregation voted in 1887 to relocate farther out at Ninth and Broadway. They began construction and occupied this building in 1894. The architect was Francis Kimball of New York, and he used the English Gothic style. The University of the South donated Sewanee stone for the building material. The chapel was built first, toward the rear of the lot, and was the first space used in 1888. The original bell from the Sixth and Church building was moved to the tower of the chapel in 1891. It had been cast by John Wilbank in Philadelphia in 1831. This space is now used as the parish hall. The cornerstone to the new sanctuary was laid by Bishop Charles T. Quintard on September 7, 1892. It weighs 5,555 pounds.

The windows above the reredos and altar were a gift memorializing George A. Washington. The Washingtons' tobacco plantation had the largest enslaved population in Tennessee. There are two sets of Tiffany Studios stained-glass windows in the side clerestory windows. One is in honor of the children of Mr. & Mrs. Leslie Warner, and the other was given by Elizabeth Childress Brown, wife of Tennessee governor, Confederate general, and railroad executive John C. Brown. The elaborately carved reredos, altar, pulpit, and pews were the work of Melchior Thoni of the Edgefield & Nashville Manufacturing Co. The bronze angel lectern

THIS USED TO BE: Christ Church Episcopal

NOW IT'S: Christ Church Cathedral

LOCATION: 900 Broadway

The chapel was first used in 1888 and the sanctuary in 1892. There are two Tiffany Studios stained-glass windows in the sanctuary. The tower was added in 1947.

is signed by its sculptor, C. B. Upjohn, and was cast in 1895. The baptismal font was exhibited at the International Exhibition of Industry, Science, and Art held in Edinburgh, Scotland, in 1886. The baptistery contains the only known immersion pool in an Episcopal church in Tennessee. The tower was originally planned in 1890 but not erected until 1947 under the supervision of architect Russell Hart. In 1998, Lively-Fulcher of Alexandria, Virginia, was commissioned to design a new organ and to move it into the balcony at the rear of the nave. It contains 3,370 pipes, 56 stops, and 60 ranks. On the exterior, there are gargoyles carved from Bowling Green stone. Once a parish church, it is now the cathedral of the Episcopal Diocese of Tennessee.

US Post Office

Designed as the new main US Post Office for Nashville by Marr and Holman in 1933–34, this was declared surplus by the federal government and transferred to Metro in 1999. The city paid $4.4 million for the building and also appropriated $15 million toward the renovation of the structure as an arts facility. The Frist Foundation contributed $25 million toward the renovation and to establish an endowment for the art center. Metro has granted a 99-year lease for $1 per year to the Frist Art Museum. Tuck-Hinton Architects converted it into an art center for the exhibition of rented traveling exhibitions both national and international and for in-house curation of focused exhibitions. It has moved Nashville into a new tier of exhibition sites in America with loans from national archaeological museums in Egypt, the British Museum, and numerous American and Tennessee museums. A small post office still operates out of the ground floor.

Opening in 2001, with about 24,000 square feet of exhibition space, it is an inviting and beautiful home to the art of the world. With no collection of its own, the Frist is free to delve into the art of humankind from all cultures, periods, and nations. It has an engaging and innovative children's interactive space called the Martin ArtQuest, with drawing, painting, and printmaking stations to engage young minds, eyes, and hands in the creation of art.

The building is a classicized Art Deco style. The federal government had worked with Marr and Holman a few years earlier on the construction of the Federal Reserve building on Third Avenue North, which might have helped Marr and Holmen get the contract for this marvelous Deco delight. In the postal lobby where the stamps were sold, packages picked up, and private mailboxes rented, the grilles above the clerks' windows are made of cast aluminum and feature depictions of Ford tri-motor airplanes, diesel locomotives, and other modern means of getting the mail delivered. Marble, terrazzo, and silver leaf Art Deco stenciling on the ceiling gave the space a very modern Jazz-Age feel. During World War II GIs left for the war from Union Station next door, and their letters to and from home

An Art Deco must-see lobby awaits you inside. Originally the main US Post Office, it featured an elevated covered connector to the train yard next door so that the mail could safely get into the building. Now it is an arts center with changing loan exhibitions.

came through this post office. Every April 15, last-minute income-tax filers lined up along Broadway to drop off their forms, and postal workers lined up to take the full bins inside.

THIS USED TO BE: US Post Office

NOW IT'S: Frist Art Museum

LOCATION: 919 Broadway

Union Station

Union Station was designed by L&N engineer Richard Montfort. Ground was broken for the building on August 1, 1898, and it was opened on October 9, 1900. It is in the Richardsonian Romanesque Revival style, inspired by H. H. Richardson's Allegheny County Courthouse in Pittsburgh, Pennsylvania. Union Station is clad in Bowling Green stone and has a slate roof. To the rear is a baggage, mail, and express building, which now has a brewpub in it.

The square front tower is 220 feet tall. It once had a three-dimensional statue of Mercury on the top of the tower, but a storm blew it off in 1952. It was so badly damaged by its fall that it could not be repaired. Recently, a two-dimensional version has been put back on the top of the tower. The original statue had been on the Commerce Building at the Tennessee Centennial Exposition, and Major Eugene Castner Lewis, who had it created for the exposition, so loved it that he had it cap off the new terminal for the railroad he worked for.

The old train schedule board is still in the lobby behind the hotel clerks' counter. The floor-to-ceiling rise in the lobby is 63 feet to a barrel vault of stained glass. This space measures 67 feet by 125 feet. The rail barn that was behind the building was 250 feet by 500 feet and had a clear span of 200 feet. Ten full-length trains could sit beneath it. The station is raised up to the level of a viaduct to give the valley below to the trains. Trains ran beneath the station and unloaded freight and passengers at the rear under the shelter of the train shed. The end of the shed nearest to the station had lancet windows in frosted glass, with stained-glass roundels at the tops.

THIS USED TO BE: Union Station

NOW IT'S: Union Station Nashville Yards Hotel

LOCATION: 1001 Broadway

A railroad station from 1901 to 1979, it is now a hotel. The lobby ceiling is 65 feet high, with a barrel vault of stained glass.

The station closed to freight trains in 1975, but Amtrak continued to run passenger trains from it until 1979. The building then deteriorated. Citizens concerned about this neglect got the Metropolitan government to acquire it and lease it to developers, who renovated it into a hotel and restaurants. Edwards and Hotchkiss Architects did this work. Union Station has been renovated several other times since then but is still a grand place to spend the night and to dine.

Cummins Station

Built to work in conjunction with the Union Station freight yards beside which it sat, this large warehouse and office building was built by Oliver Contracting Co. in 1906–07. Built for William J. Cummins, the chairman of the Bon Air Coal and Iron Corporation, it is 132 feet by 500 feet, with five floors, and is 480,000 square feet. Cummins Station was the first reinforced concrete building in Nashville and had a brick outer veneer. In 1907 it ranked as the world's largest concrete warehouse. The goods stored inside were safe in what was essentially a fireproof space. Local businesses such as Cheek-Neal Coffee Company (Maxwell House Coffee) and H. G. Hill grocers handled their freight needs from there.

In 1993 Henry Sender began renovations on Cummins Station, turning it into offices, shops, bars, and restaurants. That helped launch

the railyards into a new community of high-rise apartments and condominiums, restaurants, bars, and shops, making it a popular destination. Today it is a popular place to live, work, and play. Musical instruments maker Gibson Brands, Cinco De Mayo Mexican restaurant, and GS&F advertising agency all have space here. Gibson has 7,150 square feet, where musicians can select various specialty woods for guitars to customize their instruments; the shop also has a performance stage.

THIS USED TO BE: Cummins Station freight warehouse

NOW IT'S: Cummins Station shops and offices

LOCATION: 209 10th Ave. S.

Built between 1906 and 1907 as a freight transit hub, Cummins Station is now shops and offices.

Centennial Park

In 1896 Tennessee reached its 100th year as a state. But due to a national depression, there was no funding to celebrate the occasion that year. The next year, the Tennessee Centennial Exposition was held at West Side Park. The horse-racing ground was located west of town and comprised a large tract of open ground beside the L&N Railroad Roundhouse, freight yard, and workshops. So it was conveniently beside the rail lines, for easy shipment of whatever exhibitors might wish to put on display, and many firms, states, and groups did wish to participate. The exposition was modeled after the World's Columbian Exposition, held in Chicago in 1893. The White City, as that exposition's overarching design was called, inspired the Centennial Exposition here to follow the classical architectural style of that fair, and everything here was painted white as well. The State of Illinois even put up a reduced scale exhibition building following the design of the Administration Building designed by Richard M. Hunt for the Chicago fair.

A full-scale replica of the Parthenon served as an art gallery at the Tennessee exhibition, and the state put together exhibits on agriculture, commerce, industry, and transportation. The structures were designed to be temporary, and after the fair they were demolished. The Parthenon was much loved, however, and it was seen as an embodiment of Nashville's nickname, "the Athens of the South." So, the public resisted demolishing it. But by 1915, it had to be roped off as a public hazard, as plaster was falling off of it. Permanent replacement of the plaster with concrete began in 1921,

THIS USED TO BE: Tennessee Centennial Exposition grounds

NOW IT'S: Centennial Park

LOCATION: West End Avenue

First a horse-racing park, then the site of the Tennessee Centennial Exposition, this is one of the early 20th-century parks laid out in the city for public enjoyment. The replica of the Parthenon was built as the art gallery for the exposition and was so popular that it was rebuilt between 1921 and 1931 in permanent material. It is the only full-scale replica in the world of the ancient temple, and it has an art gallery in the basement.

and the Parthenon reopened in 1931. Russell Hart and William Dinsmoor were the architects of the 1931 building, with Belle Kinney Scholz and her husband, Leopold Scholz, being the sculptors of the re-creations of the pedimental sculptures. From 1986 to 1990, renovations were undertaken by Gresham, Smith & Partners, and from 1994 to 2001, exterior restoration was done.

Unfortunately, Centennial Park is also a reminder of Jim Crow-era bigotry. It had a segregated swimming pool; when the city was ordered to desegregate its swimming pools, it closed all of them instead. The sunken garden marks the spot where a swimming pool used to be.

Shelby Park

This 361-acre park sits beside the Cumberland River. In 1890 the Edgefield Company purchased some of the heavily wooded riverside tract and operated an amusement park there for a few years after the Fatherland Street/Shelby Avenue streetcar line ran out there. The park had a roller coaster, boat rides, balloon ascensions with a parachute drop, and a shooting gallery among its attractions. It also hosted picnics, dances, horseback riding, and Sunday band concerts. It eventually went bankrupt and closed. In 1909 the parks board purchased 151 acres of this woodland and 60 more acres in 1911 from J. P. Meredith. It was mostly forest-covered wilderness. From the Cumberland River back to the rolling hills beyond the river plain, the grand feature of the park was its virgin forest. It was claimed to hold numerous species of beech, sugar maple, oak, poplar, gum, walnut, hackberry, wild cherry, and hickory trees covered with vines, and forming a dense canopy. There were 72 varieties of trees and shrubs. The parks board decided at that point to preserve most of the tree canopy and to limit access to the picnic shelters and boats on Lake Sevier. The board opened access via new macadam roads, using a rock quarry opened there to provide the stone to surface five miles of park drives. Shelby Park opened to the public on July 4, 1912. Parks Commissioner M. T. Bryan declared that "in natural beauty and desirability for park purposes these grounds cannot be excelled anywhere." Mayor Hilary Howse chimed in, saying that it was "the most beautiful natural park in the southland." The park commissioners pledged "that as beauty is the chief consideration for all park drives, every effort will be made to develop the most natural

THIS USED TO BE: Shelby Amusement Park

NOW IT'S: Shelby Park

LOCATION: Shelby Ave. at Twentieth St.

The woodlands, the riverbank boat access, and the addition of Shelby Bottoms has made this one of the largest urban parks in the city. Windmill Hill was once topped with a Dutch windmill, which burned during World War II. Cave Spring is now a ruin, but its beauty can still be enjoyed.

and picturesque views around the lake and hills throughout the property that can be obtained, never defacing nature, but seeking to add charm to all points approached." Major E. C. Lewis designed numerous concrete structures for the park, including a Dutch windmill, a boathouse resembling a sidewheel steamboat in Lake Sevier, and the Cave Spring pergola. The first two are gone now, and Cave Spring is a ruin. In 1936 the WPA built a golf course. Mayor Phil Bredesen had the city purchase the adjoining Shelby Bottoms natural area, and in 2011 the city acquired the Cornelia Fort Airpark to bring the total parkland up to over 1,000 acres. There are now two golf courses in the park.

Peace Monument

James E. Caldwell and May Winston Caldwell, his wife, were both interested in the Battle of Nashville and in preserving and perpetuating the history of that battle. She led the effort to create a monument to the battle after the attempts to convince President Taft to create Franklin and Nashville battlefield parks had failed. With the Great War (World War I) having just ended, she decided to create a monument to peace. It was situated near the Caldwells' home, Longview, on Franklin Road, near where Thompson Lane dead-ended into that road. The couple commissioned Giuseppe Moretti of Italy to create the monument, and the Ladies' Battlefield Association raised the funds to pay for it. The Vaulx family donated the land for the monument, which was dedicated in 1927. The central figure represents "The Spirit of Youth" holding in check the warhorses of North and South. Overarching it on a granite shaft is the Angel of Peace. It was conceived as a memorial to Americans who died in both the Civil War and World War I. In 1974 a tornado destroyed the granite shaft and badly twisted the bronze figures. The Tennessee Historical Commission restored the bronze portion of the monument. In 1999 the monument was moved to a new base and a new location, and a re-created shaft with the Angel of Peace hovering over it was installed. The bronze sculpture was relocated to this site at that time. Both areas had been parts of the battlefield, and an oak tree that was on the battlefield is still growing there beside the Peace Monument.

Moretti, the monument's sculptor, was born in Siena, Italy, in 1857 and died in San Remo, Italy, in 1935. He began studying

THIS USED TO BE: Peace Monument at the end of Thompson Lane

NOW IT'S: Peace Monument on Granny White Pike

LOCATION: Granny White Pike between Clifton Lane and Battlefield Dr.

Erected to commemorate both the end of World War I and the reunification after the Civil War, the Peace Monument has been moved from its original location.

sculpting at the age of nine with Tito Serrochi, who had a studio in the cloister of the church in Siena. He later studied at the Academy of Fine Arts of Florence under Giovanni Dupré. He there met a Croatian sculptor, Ivan Rendić, and joined him in Zagreb at his studio to apprentice further. He later moved to Vienna, where he worked on the Rothschild palace and executed a bust of Emperor Franz Joseph that was shown at the Paris Exposition of 1900. Finally, in 1888, he decided to move to America. He worked in New York City and was hired by Richard Morris Hunt to do bas-reliefs and friezes for Hunt's construction of Marble House for William K. Vanderbilt at Newport. That led to commissions in Pittsburgh and then Birmingham, where he created the Vulcan statue. His sculpture of Commodore Cornelius Vanderbilt was commissioned by Vanderbilt University and first exhibited at the Centennial Exposition, in front of the Parthenon. It now stands in front of Kirkland Hall.

Fort Negley Park

James E. Caldwell initiated efforts to acquire the site of Fort Negley in 1913. He proposed that Capitol Boulevard be extended all the way to the fort, and that the fort be restored. Senator Luke Lea and Congressman Joe Byrns sponsored a bill in Congress to designate Fort Negley as a national park and to fund its restoration. The bill failed; however, Caldwell's son, Rogers Caldwell, was then on the Nashville parks board, and he helped to persuade the board to buy Saint Cloud Hill and the ruins of the fort as a public park in 1928.

Most of the original stone had been removed in 1889 to build the new city reservoir on Kirkpatrick Hill nearby. That hill had been the site of Fort Casino during the Civil War occupation of Nashville. Capt. James St. Clair Morton designed these fortifications in 1862, and enslaved men were forced to build the fortifications around the city. Fort Negley was the largest inland stone fortification built during the war. From August to December 1862, over 2,700 "contrabands" (runaway enslaved people) and free Blacks were forced into labor gangs to build the fort. The fort remained a federal garrison until September 1867, when the Army dismantled the fortifications around the city.

In 1936 the WPA, using plans found in the National Archives, rebuilt Fort Negley and added a driveway up and around the hill, a parking lot, and an interpretive area. Baseball fields were laid out on the flat ground at the base of the hill, and the park opened in 1938. In the 1960s, the parks department took down the wooden stockade and closed the fort area to the public. Trees overtook the hill during this period of neglect, and homeless camps occupied the area in the 1980s. In 2002 Mayor Bill Purcell got the City Council to appropriate

Watch the interpretive film in the Visitor Center, and then read the historical markers as you walk up the hill and through the fort.

The original fort was built with forced enslaved and free Black labor in 1862. It was rebuilt by the Public Works Administration in 1936 but was subsequently allowed to fall back into ruin. In 2002 it was stabilized.

funding to stabilize the ruins and build wooden pathways to protect the ruins from foot traffic. It reopened to the public in 2004. The Visitor Center opened in 2007.

THIS USED TO BE: WPA reconstruction of a Civil War fort

NOW IT'S: A partially stabilized ruin of the fort

LOCATION: Fort Negley Blvd.

City Hospital

Opening on April 23, 1890, the City Hospital had 65 beds and was the first full-fledged city-run hospital. It cost $30,000 to build. The first administrator, Dr. Charles Brower, sought the help of Charlotte E. Perkins, a head nurse in Pennsylvania, to establish a sound medical care facility for Nashville. Together they founded a nursing training school in 1891, which was the only one of its kind south of the Ohio River and north of New Orleans. That school functioned until 1970. In 1932 the central and western portions of the hospital were demolished and an Art Deco-inspired addition was put up. That brought up the daily patient capacity to 188. It was renamed General Hospital. In 1998 it merged with Meharry-Hubbard Hospital, and the Hermitage Avenue site was closed. One wing of the hospital remains in this apartment complex, and a main building that was updated in the 1940s still survives as apartments.

This building is part of a revitalization of College Hill/Rutledge Hill that began in the 1980s. The former bus repair and storage sheds have been converted into Pinewood Social, which contains a restaurant, a coffee shop, bowling lanes, pools, and a bocce court. Centric Architecture, the Entrepreneur Center, the Center for Nonprofit Management, Hands On Nashville, the Metropolitan Development and Housing Agency, and Emma use these WPA-built sheds. Ryman Lofts is another housing component on the hill. It offers affordable housing to artists.

In keeping with the plan for this area to be a mixed-use and mixed-income neighborhood, Nance Place offers workforce affordable housing units with one-, two-, and three-bedroom units. It achieved LEED status when completed.

THIS USED TO BE: City Hospital

NOW IT'S: City View Apartments

LOCATION: 500 Rolling Mill Hill Rd.

Built in 1890, City Hospital is now a condominium. In the 1940s an annex was built, and two thirds of the original building was pulled down.

Next door, to the south, was the site of the Tennessee School for the Blind established in 1844. It ran a segregated school next door in a separate building for African Americans. That structure still stands and dates to 1944. It was designed by Donald Southgate, a prominent local white architect. In 1965 the two blind schools merged, and soon thereafter they moved out to Donelson. Now Metro is slated to purchase the land for the parks system.

Check out the view of the city from the overlook on the bluff edge.

Fisk University

The Fisk Free Colored School was one of the first institutions dedicated to educating newly freed enslaved people after the Civil War. It was founded a few months after the war's conclusion by John Ogden, Rev. Erastus Milo Cravath, and Rev. Edward P. Smith, with the support of the American Missionary Association, the Freedmen's Aid Commission, and the Freedmen's Bureau. It was named in honor of Union general Clinton B. Fisk, the assistant commissioner of the Freedmen's Bureau of Tennessee.

At first, the school was located in a former military barracks near Union Station. The first classes were held on January 9, 1866, with students ranging in age from 7 to 70. All had endured enslavement and poverty, and they were eager to gain an education. The school later moved to the site of the former Fort Gillem. The oldest structure on campus is the Little Theater, a former Union Army hospital barracks.

The school, which had become Fisk University, was struggling financially in 1871, and a touring choral group called the Jubilee Singers was formed to raise money for it. George L. White was Fisk's treasurer and music teacher. He put together five women and four men as a trial tour group. The name he came up with is from Leviticus 25, when the Hebrews are instructed to celebrate the year of Jubilee to mark the anniversary of being delivered from bondage. The group toured nationally and internationally and even performed before Queen Victoria. It raised $150,000, enough to repay the purchase price for the land and to pay for the construction of Jubilee Hall. That building was put up between 1873 and 1876. Stephen D. Hatch of New York designed it. The wainscoting in the front halls is wood brought from the Mendi Mission in West Africa. The newel post is made up of 29 different kinds of fine wood. The front door is black walnut with bronze trim. Having survived financial

Visit Jubilee Hall, Fisk Chapel, and the Van Vechten Gallery. The Van Vechten contains some of Georgia O'Keefe's gift of art to the university.

Founded as one of the first institutions to educate the newly emancipated enslaved people following the Civil War, Fisk University has a distinguished history, with many prominent alums. Ida B. Wells, James Weldon Johnson, W. E. B. Du Bois, Nikki Giovanni, John Hope Franklin, John Lewis, and Diane Nash were among those who have passed through here.

hard times and a transition from a white administration and faculty to an integrated staff and student body, Fisk is one of the leading historically Black colleges and universities in America. Jubilee Hall is a National Historic Landmark.

THIS USED TO BE: Fisk Free Colored School

NOW IT'S: Fisk University

LOCATION: Jefferson St. at Dr. D. B. Todd Blvd.

Scarritt College for Christian Workers

Designed by Henry C. Hibbs in the mid-1920s, this is one of two campuses in this style that he designed in Tennessee. The other one is what had been Southwestern at Memphis and is now Rhodes College. He used Crab Orchard stone and Indiana limestone in their construction and employed the Collegiate Gothic style of architecture. They are the best examples of that style in the state. In 1929 Hibbs's work received the AIA Gold Medal.

The school began in 1892 as Scarritt Bible and Training School in Kansas City, Missouri. Belle Harris Bennett founded it as a training school for missionaries. Martha Matilda Chick Scarritt of Kansas City, the child of missionaries to India, made the first pledge. In 1924, the school was moved to Nashville.

The Belle Harris Bennett Memorial, which included Scarritt Hall, Bennett Hall, Wightman Chapel, and the tower, as well as the Susie Gray Dining Hall, opened in 1927. They were patterned after the dining halls at Oxford University. In 1928 the Belle Harris Bennett complex was built. It connected the administration and social buildings, along with Wightman Chapel. Wightman Chapel was named for Marcia Davies Wightman, a women's-rights activist from Louisiana. The Gothic tower that Hibbs designed was the tallest building in Nashville at that time at 115 feet. It became the symbol for the campus. The school was located beside Peabody College for Teachers in order to link the two in the instruction of Christian educators and church music programs. Beginning in the 1930s, the college offered bachelor's degrees and graduate education in community and family service, social work, and religious education. Between 1940 and into the 1960s, the campus grew, with six other buildings being added. In 1952 the first two African American students were admitted, Lelia Robinson and DeLaris Johnson, making Scarritt the first private, predominately white college to desegregate in Tennessee. Dr. Martin Luther King Jr. spoke at the school on April 25, 1957.

This Collegiate Gothic complex is the work of Henry Clossen Hibbs, who was a master in this style and in Romanstyle architectural forms. It is now a United Methodist Women's conference and retreat center.

In 1973 J. Richard Palmer, from Berea College, was installed as president. He was tasked with increasing enrollment and raising money, but he resigned in 1977 due to administration politics.

By 1988 enrollment had dropped to such a small number that the United Methodist Church, the school's patron, sold it to the United Methodist Women. It is now a nonprofit conference, retreat, and education center.

THIS USED TO BE: The Scarritt College for Christian Workers

NOW IT'S: Scarritt Bennett Center, a nonprofit conference, retreat, and education center

LOCATION: 1027 18th Ave. S.

Renraw

Built as the home of Mary Ann Childress, the daughter of Zachariah Stull, in 1855, this home was purchased around 1886 by James C. Warner as a country retreat. Warner named the home by spelling his own name backward. There was a large dining room downstairs with two dining tables and two sideboards, and the Warners had their bedroom on the first floor, with seven more bedrooms and two baths upstairs. The well was so deep that when it was drilled, blind cave fish came up with the water. For drinking water the Warners used a cistern. In the 1890s, extensive alterations and additions, including the porte cochere, were made.

When James C. Warner died in 1895, his son Percy Warner; Percy's wife, Margaret; and their children made Renraw their permanent residence. They removed the partition to the downstairs bedroom at that time, creating a large drawing room. The property had a sulky racing track. In 1904 daughters Sadie and Mary Louise had their coming-out party at the home. The Warners sold the property in 1913.

Trevecca College then purchased the property to serve as its new campus. The school was established in 1901 by Cumberland Presbyterian minister J. O. McClurkan as the Pentecostal Literary and Bible Training School for Christian Workers. Its first home was the old Hynes School, which had been a men's VD hospital during the Civil War. The school changed its name in 1910 when it started offering bachelor's degrees.

THIS USED TO BE: Renraw

NOW IT'S: Lincoln Tech

LOCATION: 1524 Gallatin Ave.

Once the country retreat of James C. Warner, this then became the country home of Percy Warner and other family members. In time Trevecca College moved here, then the Nashville Auto Diesel College, and now Lincoln Tech.

In 1917 the campus had a devastating fire, and the college relocated for a time to Ruskin Cave College near Dickson, Tennessee. That same year it became an official Church of the Nazarene college to save itself financially. It merged with the Southeastern Nazarene College of Georgia, but in 1932 the school declared bankruptcy and sold the Renraw campus. It is now located on Murfreesboro Pike. Nashville Auto Diesel College then moved onto the campus. The school was later purchased by Lincoln Tech.

Belmont Mansion

In 1839 Adelicia Hayes married Isaac Franklin, the largest slave trader in America. His human trafficking had made him immensely wealthy. He owned what ultimately was divided into six plantations on 8,700 acres at the confluence of the Mississippi and Red rivers in Louisiana. He also had 10,000 acres in Texas, and Fairvue, his plantation in Sumner County. He died in Louisiana in 1846, and under his will, if Adelicia remarried, her inheritance would be cut off. Her father decided to try to break the will in Louisiana, where under the Napoleonic Code, women had property rights, unlike under the laws in the rest of the country. They won, and she was now fabulously rich. Adelicia Hayes Franklin acquired the land here in 1849 prior to her second marriage to Joseph Acklen. It is believed that work began on the house around 1853. The Acklens moved into the home about 1855, and in 1858 they hired Adolphus Heiman to enlarge the home into the grandest estate in Tennessee. The home occupied 10,900 square feet and had 36 rooms, with two one-story wings to the front of the mansion. These wings were heavily ornamented with cast-iron balconies on three sides and cast-iron cresting along the roofline. The main block was two stories high and had a recessed porch with massive fluted Corinthian columns at the center and pilasters. The house was crowned with a cupola. The grounds were the most elaborate private estate in Tennessee. There were five cast-iron gazebos, a cast-iron aviary, a zoo, stables, an art gallery, and a 300-foot-long greenhouse with a 105-foot-tall water tower to supply the gardens with water.

THIS USED TO BE: Belmont Mansion

NOW IT'S: Belmont University

LOCATION: 1900 Belmont Blvd.

Built as a summer estate, the Belmont Mansion was the finest home in antebellum Nashville and even into the post-war years. It had the largest landscaped grounds in the state, with a private zoo, art gallery, bowling alley, plunge bath, greenhouse, and water tower. Some of the grounds survive, as does the house. It is a must-see. Now it is on a campus quadrangle of Belmont University, one of the fastest-growing universities in Tennessee. Top photo courtesy of Ed Houk.

Adelicia sold the estate in 1887 and moved to Washington, DC, where her oldest son was in Congress. It became Belmont Junior College, then Ward-Belmont College, and since 1951 Belmont University. Such famous women as Clare Boothe Luce, Mary Martin, and Ophelia Colley Cannon (a.k.a. Minnie Pearl) went to school at Ward-Belmont. The campus has more than doubled its number of schools and buildings in the last 10 years.

Tennessee A&I

This was Tennessee's first segregated state public school for the higher education of African Americans. Opened in 1912 as Tennessee Agricultural and Industrial State Normal School for Negroes, it initially opened with three buildings: the Administration Building, the men's dorm, and the women's dorm. They were designed in a restrained Collegiate Gothic style and have all been replaced. In 1925 its name was shortened to Tennessee Agricultural and Industrial State Normal College. In 1927 Hale Hall, the original library, and Harned Science Hall were being built. During the Great Depression, the architects Marr and Holman designed the Jane E. Elliott Women's Building. Tisdale and Pinson designed the Administration and Health Building in a Colonial Revival style with a cupola on top. The school's motto, "Think, Work, Serve," is carved over the entrance. Local distinguished African American architects McKissack & McKissack designed the Industrial Arts Building. Under the New Deal, the landscaping of the campus was expanded, and a football stadium was built. In 1941 the state legislature directed the Board of Education to upgrade the educational programing at the school. By 1944 the school was offering its first master's degree, and in 1946 it was fully accredited by the Southern Association of Colleges and Schools.

Between 1943 and 1968 President Walter S. Davis constructed what then would be 70 percent of the campus facilities and established the graduate school and four other schools. In 1978, under a desegregation court order, the University of Tennessee–Nashville merged with TSU, and now it gives minority scholarships to

THIS USED TO BE: Tennessee Agricultural and Industrial State Normal School for Negroes

NOW IT'S: Tennessee State University

LOCATION: 1005 Dr. D. B. Todd Jr. Blvd.

Created as a segregated African American normal school, it has transformed since desegregation and is a thriving university located close to Fisk University and Meharry Medical College.

non-African Americans. Oprah Winfrey is a graduate, as is Olympian Wilma Rudolph.

With the most land of any college campus in Nashville, the main campus sits on 500 acres. The Avon Williams Campus is downtown, near the Tennessee State Capitol. The school ranks 34th among historically Black colleges and universities in the *U.S. News & World Report* survey. It awards 38 baccalaureate degrees, 24 master's degrees, and doctoral degrees in seven areas (biological sciences, computer information systems engineering, psychology, public administration, curriculum and instruction, educational administration and supervision, and physical therapy), as well as two associate's degrees, one in nursing and one in dental hygiene.

George Peabody College for Teachers

The Davidson Academy was established in 1785 as the first educational institution in Nashville. The school moved into the city in 1806 and rechartered itself as Cumberland College in 1826. The next year the name was changed to the University of Nashville. Dr. Philip Lindsley, the acting president of Princeton University, came here to head up the new school. His son, John Berrien Lindsley, founded a medical school attached to the university. In 1875 the Peabody Education Fund gave the school the funds to become a teachers' college. At that time, Montgomery Bell Academy, a school for boys; the medical school; and the literary arts department were all spun off as independent entities. The medical school was moved to Vanderbilt University. The state legislature amended the charter of the school to accomplish this. In 1889 the University of Nashville was renamed Peabody Normal School.

Originally located in South Nashville, the campus moved to 21st Avenue South in 1914. Dr. Bruce Payne was the president of the school at that time, and he consciously copied the University of Virginia plan of a domed building flanked by classically inspired structures running down a slope on an open-ended mall. Ludlow and Peabody of Boston were the first architects from 1913 to 1915. They designed the Social and Religious Building and the Psychology, Industrial Arts, and Home Economics buildings. The new library followed in 1918–19, designed by Edward Tilton.

Classicism continued to be the design choice of McKim, Mead and White in the 1920s with the addition of the administration building, the Peabody Demonstration School (today's University School), and the Cohen Fine Arts Building. Henry Hibbs added east and west dormitories, and Raymond Hood the graduate dormitory. Granberry Jackson Jr. added the last Classical Revival building, which was named for Payne.

In 1950 Warfield and Associates built a modernist student center, breaking the classical mold on the campus. In 1968 Warterfield and Bass designed the Human Development Laboratory, and Street & Street added the Mental Retardation Laboratory. Peabody merged

Relocated in 1914 from the old University of Nashville campus in south Nashville to this Hillsboro Road/21st Avenue South site, the campus is patterned after Thomas Jefferson's design for the University of Virginia. In 1979 it was absorbed by Vanderbilt University, which is located across the street.

with Vanderbilt University in 1979, and in 2006–08 the Commons Center was added, with five new dormitories designed by Bruner/Cott of Cambridge, Massachusetts. It received a Gold Level LEED certification for environmentally sustainable design. The Peabody campus is a National Historic Landmark.

THIS USED TO BE: George Peabody College for Teachers

NOW IT'S: Peabody College of Vanderbilt University

LOCATION: 21st Ave. South at Edgehill Ave.

Church of the Advent

Bishop James Hervey Otey established the Episcopal Church in Tennessee in 1829 by founding Christ Church parish in Nashville. The congregation followed the established practice of renting pews to parishioners. This generated the funds needed to operate the church. Charles Tomes came to town in 1848 to be Christ Church's rector and married Bishop Otey's daughter. The bishop and his son-in-law saw that the free pews were overflowing, while the rented pews often sat empty. They wished to end the rental system. They called for a vote, but lost when eight families blocked it from passing. Tomes led those who wished to end this system to withdraw from Christ Church and to form the Church of the Advent. The split was not his idea, but he accepted the call to become the new church's first rector. He died suddenly, though, before he had even had an opportunity to preach there. Dr. Charles Quintard was called in 1857 and became the rector. He went on to become the bishop of Tennessee.

Designed by architect Robert Sharp and built in 1910 as the Episcopal Church of the Advent, this building has made many transitions in its useful life. The congregation had moved to the suburban neighborhood from Seventh and Commerce. The Reverend Walter E. Dakin, the grandfather of Thomas Lanier "Tennessee" Williams, was a rector at this church. Young "Tennessee" would visit his grandparents here as a very young child, and his African American nurse, Ozzie, "would take us to the park on summer days and we would sit under the trees while she read us some ghost stories and made up others. And then I would go home at nap time and make up more stories while I was going to sleep."

THIS USED TO BE: Episcopal Church of the Advent

NOW IT'S: Ocean Way Studio

LOCATION: 1200 17th Ave. S.

Tennessee Williams spent part of his childhood here with his grandfather, who was the rector. Now it is a recording studio.

The church moved out to Franklin Road in 1973. It briefly served as the YMCA's "Urban Village." Then the Tennessee Performing Arts Center acquired it for offices and a theater space. It was purchased by Tony Alamo for his business, and then in 1995 it was remodeled as a modern recording studio. Belmont University bought the building in 2001 and operates it as Ocean Way Studio. In 1991 the rectory annex, where Tennessee Williams had lived briefly, was damaged in a fire. It was repaired and is still part of Ocean Way.

RCA Studio A

RCA built Studio A in 1965. Harold Bradley and his brother Owen Bradley had established a recording studio of their own down the street in 1954. They attached a quonset hut to a former home to use as their studio. It was Bradley's Film & Recording Studio and was later operated by Columbia. Although it was the first recording studio on what would become Music Row. It has been demolished. The Bradleys helped Chet Atkins to plan out a new facility. This became the Nashville headquarters of RCA and was headed up by Atkins as he devised and launched "the Nashville Sound" in the 1960s. The Nashville Sound was a pop-influenced, smoother sound for country music. Here such stars as Dottie West, Porter Wagoner, Dolly Parton, Jerry Reed, Skeeter Davis, Charley Pride, Roy Orbison, Boots Randolph, the Beach Boys, Tony Bennett, Joe Cocker, Brent Cobb, Ben Folds, William Shatner, Chris Stapleton, George Strait, Zach Bryan, Paramore, Alan Jackson, Waylon Jennings, B. B. King, Miranda Lambert, Loretta Lynn, Jason Isbell, the Monkees, Leon Russell, Anita Kerr, the Jordanaires, and Ernest Tubb made recording history. Atkins was the most recorded solo instrumentalist in recording history. His style influenced such artists as the Ventures, George Harrison, and Mark Knopfler, and produced an estimated 60 percent of the Billboard Hot Country Songs chart.

This building closed as an RCA studio in 1977 but continued to be used by independent artists. Ben Folds leased it from 2002 to 2014. At that time a local developer wanted to demolish it and build condominiums on its site. Folds gathered local supporters, and Curb Records owner Mike Curb and local philanthropists Chuck

THIS USED TO BE: RCA Studio A

NOW IT'S: RCA Studio A

LOCATION: 30 Music Square W.

Chet Atkins's "Nashville Sound" was born here, and a who's who of performers have cut their tracks here.

Elcan and Aubrey Preston jointly purchased the building to save this historic landmark from destruction. This led to the establishment of organizations to help preserve this important musical neighborhood. The National Trust for Historic Preservation held its national conference here to help focus attention on the effort.

No longer an RCA recording studio, it is still used by various artists to record where great performers have for 60 years.

RCA Studio B

This studio was built in 1957, after Chet Atkins had become RCA Music's director of operations in Nashville. It is a simple concrete-block building built according to plans drawn up by Bill Miltenburg for offices and a recording studio. This historic structure eventually became one of the most important musical heritage sites. Dan Maddox built it for $37,525. Elvis Presley, the Everly Brothers, Waylon Jennings, Bobby Bare, Dolly Parton, Jim Reeves, Willie Nelson, Floyd Cramer, Jim Ed Brown, the Browns, Jerry Byrd, Charlie Daniels, Luderin Darbone, Skeeter Davis, Donna Fargo, Fred Foster, Don Gibson, Mickey Gilley, Bobby Goldsboro, Billy Grammer, George Hamilton IV, John Hartford, Homer and Jethro, Norma Jean, Grandpa Jones, Hank Locklin, Roger Miller, Roy Orbison, Charley Pride, Boots Randolph, Jerry Reed, Don Schlitz, Connie Smith, Hank Snow, Gary Stewart, Marty Stuart, Conway Twitty, Porter Wagoner, and Dottie West all recorded here. Such hits as Gibson's "Oh Lonsome Me," the Browns' "The Three Bells," and Jim Reeves's "He'll Have to Go" were recorded here.

The background vocals and strings that are a hallmark of the "Nashville Sound" were developed here, as was the "Nashville number system," a shorthand notation of the chord structure of a song that allowed individual parts to be created while maintaining the song's integrity. RCA sold both studios in 1977. Dan and Margaret Maddox purchased Studio B then, and they allowed the Country Music Hall of Fame and Museum to give tours of the building. In 1992 they donated it to the Hall of Fame. In 2002 the Mike Curb Foundation

THIS USED TO BE: RCA Studio B

NOW IT'S: RCA Studio B

LOCATION: 1611 Roy Acuff Pl.

This was Chet Atkins's first recording studio for RCA.

purchased it. They have leased the building in perpetuity to the Hall of Fame, which still uses it for tours. The 1970s exterior has been renovated, with the interior being returned to its analog 1970s-era prime as a "temple of sound."

No longer an RCA property, it is a recording studio that is open for tours.

Acuff-Rose Publishing Co.

The Acuff-Rose Publishing Company building was the last home to the publishing company founded in 1942 by country music performer Roy Acuff and Fred Rose, a major songwriter and music-industry figure. Rose was also known to be a great music talent scout. Rose had played piano for the Paul Whiteman band. He gave up a popular WSM Radio show in 1938 and moved to Hollywood. There he wrote songs for Gene Autry movies. He returned to Nashville and a radio show in 1942, when Autry joined the Army Air Corps. Knowing both people at WSM, home to the Grand Ole Opry radio show, and the performers with the Grand Ole Opry, he was uniquely positioned to launch a music publishing company. When Acuff approached him about teaming up, an industry was launched in Nashville.

The company published works by such performers as Hank Williams Sr., Roy Orbison, the Everly Brothers, Don Gibson, and Tom T. Hall. Acuff-Rose was the first country music publisher in Nashville and released such hits as "Oh, Pretty Woman," "Walkin' after Midnight," "Tennessee Waltz," "Your Cheatin' Heart," and "Cathy's Clown."

When they formed their partnership, Acuff and Rose promised that "our company would be honest. The writers would always be taken care of. No one would act in a shady way." Many singer/songwriters had been cheated by agents, attorneys, record labels, and record promoters. Williams proved himself to Rose in 1946 by writing "A Mansion on the Hill" while Rose stepped out for a cup of coffee. Many hits followed after that signing, such as "Jambalaya," "I'm So Lonesome I Could Cry," and "Hey Good Lookin'." Upon Rose's death in 1954, his son Wesley Rose became president, and he served in that capacity for 30 years. He helped to lead the growth of country music

This was the greatest music publishing house of country music.

One of the most important music publishing companies in its day, this is an iconic building where Hank Williams, Roy Orbison, the Everly Brothers, Don Gibson, and Tom T. Hall all published their music.

both in America and abroad. Lefty Frizzell, Felice and Boudleaux Bryant, Mickey Newbury, the Everly Brothers, Orbison, Gibson, Whitey Shafer, and Dallas Frazier were some of the songwriters that he signed for Acuff-Rose.

The company affiliated with BMI and ASCAP. In 1985 Gaylord Entertainment purchased Acuff-Rose's music catalog. Needing money for one of its hotels then under construction, it sold the catalog in 2002 to Sony/ATV Music Publishing.

The building is now the home of the Church at Avenue South, affiliated with Brentwood Baptist Church. There are now seven regional campuses of this Christian mission.

THIS USED TO BE: Acuff -Rose Publishing Co.

NOW IT'S: The Church at Avenue South

LOCATION: 2510 8th Ave. S.

The Hermitage

The Hermitage, home of President Andrew Jackson, was built in 1819. The Jacksons moved into a log blockhouse at the back of this property in 1804. Then in 1819 they began the construction on a large, two-story brick house, which they completed in 1821. The Jacksons raised cotton with the work of 50 enslaved people, which in time more than doubled. In 1834, while Jackson was serving as president, the Hermitage caught fire from a spark from the chimney and was gutted to a shell. As Jackson's second term as president was nearing its end in 1836, Joseph Reiff and William Hume were finishing their rebuilding and expansion of the house. Jackson died in 1845, and his wife's nephew, their adopted son, inherited the farm. By 1850 it comprised 1,000 acres and had 137 enslaved people working on it. Always a poor businessman, Andrew Jackson Jr. sold the house and 500 acres to the State of Tennessee in 1856. He then moved to Mississippi. The house began to fall into disrepair. Shortly before the Civil War he was invited to return as caretaker and did so. The Union troops guarded the former president's home from being pillaged during the war, probably because of his toast to John C. Calhoun: "Our Federal Union, it must be preserved!" Tragically, in 1865 Andrew Jackson Jr. died in a hunting accident. His widow, Sarah, lived on at the Hermitage until her death in 1888.

The following year, the Ladies Hermitage Association was formed to manage the property and to restore and interpret it for the state. Andrew Jackson III had removed all the furnishings and property from the house at that time. Over the years, the Ladies Hermitage Association has worked to return the house to its condition and

THIS USED TO BE: The Hermitage

NOW IT'S: Andrew Jackson's the Hermitage

LOCATION: 4580 Rachel's Lane

Home of President Andrew Jackson, it was built in 1819, expanded in 1834, and became state property in 1856. Since 1889 the Ladies Hermitage Association has administered the property for the state and run it as a house museum.

appearance when President Jackson lived in it. They have largely succeeded in reacquiring those pieces over the years. The home is open for touring, as are Tulip Grove and the old Hermitage Presbyterian Church. The visitor's center has an interpretive film, museum, and shop. This is a National Historic Landmark.

President Jackson was a complicated man. He advocated for and enacted a plan to remove Native peoples from the Southeast, a plan that went all the way to Thomas Jefferson and which was carried out by President Martin Van Buren. He also enslaved people to work on his farm. Both of these were widely held practices and beliefs that we now repudiate.

Belle Meade Plantation

Belle Meade was the home of John Harding and his son William Giles Harding. The son had been born in the old Dunham cabin beside Richland Creek, and as the farm expanded in size and prospered they built a new two-story brick house, two rooms over two rooms with a central hall. By 1820—when the brick house went up—the farm covered 1,000 acres and was home to nearly 50 enslaved people.

Young William Giles Harding went to school at the American Literary, Scientific, and Military Institute in Connecticut in 1829. He married and had two sons while living on one of his father's holdings on the Stones River. That wife, Selena McNairy, died, and he moved back home to Belle Meade. In 1839, the father moved into town and gave his son the plantation to run himself. In 1840, William married Elizabeth McGavock, and they had two daughters. By 1853 they had doubled the depth of the house by adding two more rooms over two others onto the front. They also added a massive stone portico. The shafts are made up of two pieces of quarried limestone each. By this time the plantation covered 4,000 acres. Various crops and livestock were raised there, and a 400-acre deer park was created with herds of deer and buffalo.

With the coming of the Civil War, Harding, who was a brigadier general in the Tennessee militia, gave financial support to aid the Confederacy. When the city was conquered, he was arrested for treason and was imprisoned at Fort Mackinac, Michigan. He was released after taking an oath of allegiance to the United States, and he returned to Belle Meade. During the Battle of Nashville, Brig. Gen. James R. Chalmers's Confederate forces were camped on the property and were driven off by a Federal maneuver that started with a cavalry sweep from west of town along the river, then swinging south and east, driving Confederate forces back to the Hillsboro Pike. During this skirmish, Harding's daughter Selene ran out onto the front porch and waved her handkerchief to the Confederate troops to encourage them. The front columns of the house were pockmarked with Federal bullets as a result of this, and they still show the scars today.

Tour the house, but do not miss the carriage collection and the grounds.

The site of the premier thoroughbred horse stud farm in the 19th century, it has been a house museum since 1953.

In 1868, Selene married former Confederate general William Hicks Jackson. He helped to run Belle Meade, and eventually, after William Giles Harding's death in 1886, Jackson was in sole charge of it. Harding and Jackson built up the thoroughbred stud farm into the finest in the country. Such horses as Man o' War, Iroquois, Citation, and Seattle Slew are descended from that bloodline. In 1903, after Jackson's death, the farm went bankrupt, and the land was purchased to be developed into an exclusive neighborhood for the wealthy elite of Nashville. In 1953 it was purchased by the State of Tennessee, and today Belle Meade is open to the public for tours.

THIS USED TO BE: Belle Meade Plantation

NOW IT'S: Belle Meade Historic Site & Winery

LOCATION: 5025 Harding Rd.

Tennessee State Capitol

The Tennessee State Capitol was designed by William Strickland and is a National Historic Landmark. Erected between 1845 and 1859, it is in the Greek Revival style. Strickland was convinced that it was his finest work, so much so that he is buried within the northeast corner of the building. The building chairman, Samuel Dold Morgan, is buried in the southeast corner. President and Mrs. James K. Polk are buried on the front lawn, beneath a monument design by Strickland as well. Nashville has been the permanent seat to Tennessee government since 1843. The legislature first met in this building while it was under construction in 1853 and has met there ever since.

This is where Tennessee voted to leave the United States and secede in 1861. It is where, upon Tennessee's reentering the United States, the 14th Amendment to the US Constitution was ratified and African Americans became citizens in 1868. The 15th Amendment then gave African American men the right to vote in 1870. In 1920, Tennessee was the last hope for women to gain the right to vote. Thirty-six states were needed to ratify the amendment, and 35 had voted to do so when the Tennessee General Assembly was called upon to vote on this question by Governor A. H. Roberts. Of the 12 remaining states, most were firmly against women voting. The lobbying efforts of everyone in the country on both sides were then focused upon Tennessee's General Assembly. When Banks Turner and Harry Burn changed their votes and supported women's suffrage, the issue was decided. So approximately 57 percent of today's population can vote due to action taken by the Tennessee General Assembly.

Three entities have moved out of the building. The Tennessee Historical Society left in the 1880s and took all of its collections to the Watkins Institute. In the 1920s the state took those collections into a trust agreement with the society, and it has maintained them ever since. They are now housed at the Tennessee State Museum and

Take a tour Monday through Friday. It is closed on weekends and holidays.

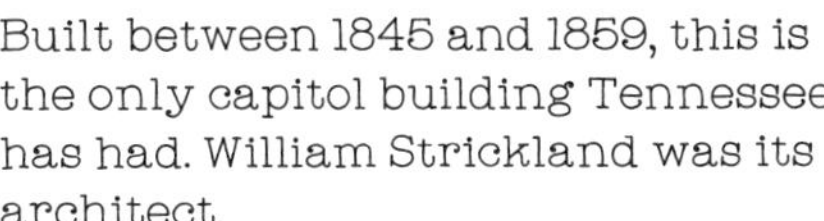
Built between 1845 and 1859, this is the only capitol building Tennessee has had. William Strickland was its architect.

the Tennessee State Library and Archives. In 1937 the Tennessee Supreme Court moved into their own building behind the Capitol on Seventh Avenue North. In 1953 the Tennessee State Library and Archives also moved out and into its own building behind the Capitol and beside the Supreme Court. The Library and Archives and the museum are now both in new buildings at the north end of the Bicentennial Capitol Mall State Park. Both the former Supreme Court chamber and the former State Library were restored in 1986 in the Capitol building. So while some government bodies have left the building, the legislature, governor, treasurer, comptroller, and secretary of state are all still working out of one of the oldest still-functioning state capitols in America.

THIS USED TO BE: Tennessee State Capitol

NOW IT'S: Tennessee State Capitol, minus the Tennessee Supreme Court, the Tennessee State Library & Archives, and the Tennessee Historical Society offices and exhibits

LOCATION: Sixth Avenue North at Charlotte Ave. (Dr. Martin Luther King Jr. Blvd.)

Far Hills

This house was built between 1929 and 1931 by William Ridley Wills I. The insurance company executive built a large Georgian home on acreage outside Nashville. The site was wooded, with a gently sloping yard going down to the street. The red brick and limestone structure is two stories high, with seven bays over seven on the main block and two areas for casual entertaining in flanking attached pavilions. The one on the left is an open-air covered porch, and the one on the other side is an enclosed, tile-floored garden room. Russell Hart, who had studied at the École des Beaux-Arts in Paris, masterfully detailed this home. A curved grand staircase is to the right as you enter the foyer. A screen of columns divides this space into an entry, with a staircase to the bedrooms upstairs, and a seating area opening onto the loggia facing the front lawn.

In 1948 the state purchased the house as its third residence to house the governors of Tennessee. Gordon Browning was the first governor to live there; his portrait is in the house, as is a portrait of the second governor to live there, Frank G. Clement. The house deteriorated over the years; because it was the governor's residence, it could not be closed for the changing out of the 1930s HVAC system, electrical upgrades, handicapped access, increased security systems, or the addition of more room to entertain. The roof leaked so badly that one night when Governor Ned McWherter went upstairs to go to bed, the ceiling had collapsed onto his bed. He checked himself into a motel.

When Governor Phil Bredesen was elected to office, he already had a lovely home in Nashville. This allowed his wife, Andrea Conte, to undertake the restoration of the home. Private funds were raised, and the HVAC was updated, the slate roof was replaced, the

Tours are available by appointment online, Tuesday and Thursday, mid-March through mid-November. Go to tn.gov and Tennessee Residence to book one.

The Tennessee Executive Residence was built as a private home in 1931. In 1948 the state purchased it, and every governor since then has lived there.

knob-and-tube wiring was updated, the windows were replaced, an elevator was installed, and a modern kitchen was put in. There still was the matter of entertaining more than 18 people at dinner without needing a tent. To solve this problem, Conservation Hall was built. It is sunk into the hill out front and has a grand staircase leading down into it, as well as an elevator. There are restrooms, a greenroom, a caterer's kitchen, a sunken garden and light well, and a large events room for meetings, receptions, and seated dinners. An elevator connects this to the house so that the governor can come down directly into a hallway leading to the events room. The slates from the old roof were given to artists, and Sherri Warner Hunter used some to make a sculpture for the atrium. Ben Caldwell made an American flag out of the copper downspouts. Limestone was given to Scott Wise, and he made a sculpture out of it. Bets Ramsey used some of the curtain and upholstery fabric to make wall hangings. And Alfred Sharp made a coffee table out of black walnut and tulip poplar wood from the site. So conservation was definitely a key part in the building of the new 2,800-square-foot entertainment space. The once-private home now has an expanded public use. The home is open on a limited basis for public tours.

THIS USED TO BE: Far Hills, a private residence

NOW IT'S: The Tennessee Executive Residence, the home to Tennessee's governors

LOCATION: 882 S. Curtiswood Ln.

Marathon Motor Works

The first component of this complex of buildings was the 1881 Nashville Cotton Mills, with additions being added in 1885 and 1887. The building has a four-story Italianate tower with quoining, curved window hoods, and two bracketed cornices. The factory had 600 employees. The 1893 depression forced a reorganization into the Phoenix Cotton Mills which lasted until only 1908.

William Henry Collier wanted to build entire cars, not just their components. He convinced Southern Engine and Boiler Works to allow him to do that in 1907. The company announced its first model that year, and in 1909 it announced two new models. Each had a four-cylinder engine with 35 horsepower. The A9 was a touring car with five seats, and the B9 was a roadster with a rumble seat. They both sold for $1,500. Twenty cars were produced in 1907, and 400 in 1909.

In 1910 A. H. Robinson, a Nashville businessman, purchased the Marathon automobile division of the Southern Engine and Boiler Works, which was located in Jackson, Tennessee. He moved the car division into the former cotton mill. The company produced over 5,000 cars over the next three years. In 1912 it expanded its footprint with a new office and showroom and added 40,000 square feet to the factory. At its peak the company produced 10,000 vehicles a year. But a constantly changing board of directors and unwise business decisions closed the factory in 1915.

After the building had been abandoned for many years, Barry L. Walker purchased the property. He wished to create a multi-use space for artists, businesses, and entertainment. At first it was an outpost in an area of drugs and prostitution. Brave and struggling artists

THIS USED TO BE: The 1881 Nasvhille Cotton Mills

NOW IT'S: Marathon Village

LOCATION: 1200–1310 Clinton St.

leased space there. In time it gained HVAC, security, and tenants. Today Walker has revitalized a blighted area with a distillery, shops, a performance hall, and an outpost of Antique Archaeology. Walker was determined to locate a Marathon automobile, and he now has several of them. One has been generously loaned to the nearby Tennessee State Museum. Four others can be seen in the original showroom on the Marathon property.

Woodlawn

Woodlawn was the home of Willoughby Williams and was built in 1822. A Palladian-style home, reminiscent of Middleton Place near Charleston, South Carolina, it had a central two-story block with oval windows on the second floor, and Palladian windows on the ground floor. Two one-story wings connected to two flanking two-story pavilions. Hugh Roland was employed to design the home. He also designed the Masonic Hall and Christ Church around this same time. John Nichols had hired the architect, and when his daughter Nancy married Williams, a successful local merchant, the house was transferred to them. Williams added the two wings to accommodate his growing family. Williams served at one time as the president of the Bank of Tennessee. He eventually owned 1,800 acres on Richland Creek. By 1850, there were 111 enslaved people working on the farm and by the 1850s Williams was spending more time on his Arkansas property, and his son John Henry Williams came to live in the house with his wife, Elizabeth; their child; and his youngest brother, Andrew. Andrew was killed during the Civil War and the house was ransacked during the skirmishing on the first day of the Battle of Nashville. John died in 1893, and the property was divided among his heirs. The house was sold out of the family in 1900 to Duncan Kenner who sold it in 1916 to Henry B. Richardson. That same year, the eastern wing and pavilion were demolished when Woodmont Boulevard was built, and new columns were added to that side of the house, making it the new front to the home. The Young and Moore families lived in the home until the 1980s, when condominiums were built on the south lawn and the house became a law office.

THIS USED TO BE: Woodlawn Plantation

NOW IT'S: Law offices

LOCATION: 127 Woodmont Blvd.

Grassmere

Michael Dunn built a Flemish bond brick home around 1810. Following the Civil War, the house was updated with a porch, a central tiered portico, and rounded arch windows. The interior was also updated with dual parlors and Victorian woodwork. The house takes its name from William Wordsworth's poem "Home at Grassmere." There are other 19th-century structures behind the house, including a tenant house, a smokehouse, and two cemeteries. The family owned property in Cuba and made and sold concrete there.

Home to the Nashville Zoo at Grassmere, this is now a premier zoo, with a humane open space for the animals to wander about in, and with a breeding program to ensure the survival of species at risk. The home dates back to 1810 and was remodeled in the 1870s.

Maiden sisters Elise and Margaret Croft left the property to the Cumberland Science Museum in 1964 and stipulated that it was to be developed into a wildlife park. The development of the park began in 1986. Then in 1996 the museum transferred the property to Metro Government, which leases it to the private Nashville Zoo. The zoo has 6,230 animals, encompassing 339 species, and it covers about 188 acres.

THIS USED TO BE: Grassmere Farm

NOW IT'S: The Nashville Zoo at Grassmere

LOCATION: 3777 Nolensville Pike

Glen Leven

Occupied in 1857 after John Thompson's earlier home burned, this two-story brick house has beautiful cast-iron Corinthian capitals, which family tradition says were made in New Orleans. During the Battle of Nashville the house was the headquarters for Confederate general Stephen D. Lee. Following the battle, the house was used as a hospital, with an estimated 450 soldiers receiving treatment there. Beginning about 1880 the farm produced vegetables for the Maxwell House Hotel and in 2005, Susan West willed the house and 65 acres to the Land Trust for Tennessee. West died the next year, and in 2009 the Land Trust decided to retain the property and to use it as its offices. The Land Trust for Tennessee is a nonprofit that safeguards natural, scenic, and historic landscapes in the state. It was established in 1999 and has conservation easements on over 119,000 acres in over 65 counties in Tennessee. It is again raising vegetables for the five-star Hermitage Hotel, which has one of the finest dining rooms in Nashville.

The home to the Land Trust for Tennessee since 2009, the house dates to 1857 and was used during the Battle of Nashville.

Call ahead for access: (615) 244-5263.

THIS USED TO BE: Glen Leven Plantation

NOW IT'S: The Land Trust for Tennessee office

LOCATION: 4000 Franklin Rd.

Tennessee State Penitentiary

Built between 1895 and 1897 as the state's main correctional facility, it functioned in that capacity from 1898 until 1992. It contained 800 small cells, each designed to hold one inmate and followed the New York plan of no communication between inmates and isolation in individual cells. Twenty-foot-high rock walls that are three feet thick surround the prison yard. A working farm was just outside the walls. On its opening day it admitted 1,403 prisoners, nearly double its intended capacity, and it remained overcrowded throughout its existence. In 1989 the Tennessee Department of Correction opened the Riverbend Maximum Security Institution nearby. As part of the *Grubbs v. Bradley* (1983) class action suit, the federal court issued a permanent injunction forbidding this facility from ever operating again as a prison. An EF-3 tornado severely damaged it in March 2020. It has been used as a film location in *Framed*, *Nashville*, *Marie*, *Ernest Goes to Jail*, *Against the Wall*, *Last Dance*, *The Green Mile*, *The Last Castle*, and *Walk the Line*.

Opening as the state's second penitentiary in 1898, it served in that capacity until 1992. It has been used in several movies since then, and Metro is buying it from the state.

The site is closed to the public, but you can see it from the road.

THIS USED TO BE: Tennessee State Penitentiary

NOW IT'S: Metro Government is working to acquire all of this site.

LOCATION: 6404 Centennial Blvd.

Sparkman Street Bridge/Shelby Street Bridge

Built between 1907 and 1909, this was the first reinforced concrete truss bridge in America. Only the trusses on the west side remain. Howard M. Jones of Murfreesboro, Tennessee, designed this innovative support system. He had studied engineering at Vanderbilt University and then finished his degree at Union College in New York State. He worked for Nashville contractors Foster-Creighton Company. This bridge had six trusses of reinforced concrete to enable it to support streetcars and automobiles and helped to launch a building boom on the east side. Jones later designed similar bridges for Jefferson Street and Whites Creek. Both of those have been replaced. In 1998 this one was closed to automobile traffic, and it has been adapted for use as a pedestrian bridge. It has one of the best views of the city at night coming over it from the east side.

Opening in 1909, this iconic bridge is now the John Seigenthaler Pedestrian Bridge, and provides a magical view of the city by day or night.

THIS USED TO BE: Sparkman Street/Shelby Street Bridge

NOW IT'S: John Seigenthaler Pedestrian Bridge

LOCATION: 3rd Ave. S.

SOURCES

Carey, Bill. *Fortunes, Fiddles & Fried Chicken: A Nashville Business History.* Hillsboro Press, 2000.

Doyle, Don. *Nashville in the New South: 1880-1930.* University of Tennessee Press, 1985.

Doyle, Don. *Nashville Since the 1920s.* University of Tennessee Press, 1985.

Gadski, Mary Ellen. *Tennessee State Capitol: Historic Structure Report.* Mendel, Mesick, Cohen, Waite, Hall, Architects, 1986.

Graham, Eleanor. *Nashville: A Short History and Selected Buildings.* Metro Historical Commission, 1974.

Hoobler, James A. *Cities under the Gun: Images of Occupied Nashville and Chattanooga.* Rutledge Hill Press, 1986.

Hoober, James A. *A Guide to Historic Nashville, Tennessee.* History Press, 2008.

Johnson, Leland R. *The Parks of Nashville: A History of the Board of Parks and Recreation.* Parks Board, 1986.

Kreyling, Christine. *Nashville By Design: Architectural Treasures.* Forest Hills Press, 2009.

Orr, Frank, Elbridge White, Charles Warterfield, eds. *Notable Nashville Architecture 1930-1980.* Middle Tennessee A I A, 1989.

West, Carroll Van. *Nashville Architecture: A Guide to the City.* University of Tennessee Press, 2015.

Schumm, William R. *Shelby Park Past & Present: A Centennial Commemorative.* Privately Printed, 2012.

Waller, William, ed. *Nashville in the 1890s.* Vanderbilt University Press, 1970.

Waller, William, ed. *Nashville, 1900 to 1910.* Vanderbilt University Press, 1972.

Wills, Ridley, II. *Nashville Pikes: 150 Years along Franklin Pike and Granny White Pike.* Privately Printed, 2015.

Nashville Pikes: 150 Years along Hillsboro Pike. Privately Printed, 2016.

Nashville Pikes: 150 Years along Harding Pike. Privately Printed, 2017.

Nashville Pikes: 150 Years along McGavock. Lebanon, Elm Hill, Stewart's Ferry, Nashville, Murfreesborro, Shelbyville, Couchville, Antioch, and Nolensville Pikes. Privately Printed, 2020.

The Hub of the Wheel: The Old City 1780-1889. Privately Printed, 2020.

Disastrous Deaths: From the Dueling Grounds on Red River to Murder on Elm Hill Pike. Privately Printed, 2014.

Lest We Forget: Nashville's Lost Businesses and Their Stories. Privately Printed, Plumblie Media,LLC, 2013.

The Tennessean, various dates.

The Nashville Banner, various dates.

INDEX